Contents

Preface   page 9

Preface to the new edition   11

1   The reader and the medium   13

What is a play?—The set and the atmosphere—The use of space—The play as a series of impacts—Stage directions about action.

2   Sound effects   19

The quality of the sound—The buildup—The knocking on the castle gate—The knocking on the bedroom door.

3   Momentum and suspense   24

Beginnings—An argument in the street—The rhythm of progression—Rhythms in a play—Argument on a park bench—Maximum receptivity.

4   Not by words alone   31

The silence under the words—The conjurer's patter — Visual transformation—The shuffling footsteps—Visual inequalities.

5   Costume and identity   40

A quick transformation—Dual identities—Disguise— Confusion without disguise—The prostitute and her cousin.

6   Identity and character   50

The mistake of psychoanalyzing—The relationship between the parts—Falstaff—Cause and effect.

7   Irony and ambiguity   57

Irony in the forum—In the nineteenth-century parlor.

8   Mental theater   62

Where to put the stress—Mental scene-changes.

9   Silence   66

Looking for silence—How to manage without signposts—
Silence alongside speech—Silence and the contemporary
playwright—Pressures toward silence—The silent killer—
Throwing down a challenge.

10 Meaning and experience   82

What the writer wrote—What does it mean?—A
prenatal examination—The meaning and the experience—
From the root experience to the collective reaction—The
writer's intentions—What about ideas?—The general and
the particular—The generalized salesman—Waiting for
the end—Levels of communication—Games and gardens.

11 Photogenic action   97

Passive acting—Spaces between words—Movies about
actors—From place to place—What the camera choses for
you—Closing the gap—Swelling veins, big eyes, and small
sighs.

12 Play-reading as a pleasure   108

Hazel-colored hair—To sum up.

Key to extracts   111

HOW TO READ A PLAY

Ronald Hayman

Grove Press
New York

Published simultaneously in Canada
Printed in the United States of America

REVISED AND UPDATED, SEPTEMBER 1999

Library of Congress Cataloging-in-Publication Data
Hayman, Ronald, 1932-
How to read a play / Ronald Hayman. — Rev. and updated ed.
p.   cm.
Includes bibliographical references.
ISBN 0-8021-3629-X
1. Drama—Study and teaching.   2. Reading.   I. Title.
PN1701.H38   1999
808.2—dc21   99-31432
CIP

Grove Press
841 Broadway
New York, NY 10003

00 01 02   10 9 8 7 6 5 4 3 2

Acknowledgments

Acknowledgments and thanks are due to the following for permission to quote from published works:
Faber & Faber Ltd and New Directions, New York, for an extract by Ezra Pound in William Carlos Williams's *Paterson;* Oxford University Press for extracts from Anton Chekhov's *Three Sisters* and *The Cherry Orchard,* in *The Oxford Chekhov,* translated and edited by Ronald Hingley; Secker & Warburg Ltd and The Viking Press for an extract from *Death of a Salesman,* printed in *Collected Plays* by Arthur Miller © 1949, renewed 1977 by Arthur Miller; Edward Albee, Jonathan Cape Ltd, and Coward, McCann & Geoghegan Inc., for an extract from *Zoo Story* in *Zoo Story and Other Plays;* ACTAC (Theatrical & Cinematic) Ltd for extracts from a statement by Harold Pinter, first appearing as "Between the Lines" in *The Sunday Times,* March 4, 1962, and revised in *The New British Drama,* Grove Press, 1964; Secker & Warburg Ltd for an extract from August Strindberg's *The Father,* translated by Michael Meyer; Eyre Methuen for extracts from Bertolt Brecht's *Life of Galileo* and *The Good Person of Szechwan,* translated by Marsh and Brooks and John Willett respectively, © 1955 by Suhrkamp Verlag Berlin, and © D. Vesey 1960 and John Willett 1962 respectively, and for extracts from Harold Pinter's *The Caretaker* and *The Birthday Party;* International Copyright Bureau Ltd for an extract from Nikolai Gogol's *The Government Inspector,* translated by Marsh and Brooks; Hart-Davis MacGibbon Ltd for an extract from Henrik Ibsen's *Hedda Gabler,* translated by Michael Meyer; J. M. Dent and Sons Ltd for an extract from Henrik Ibsen's *Rosmersholm,* translated by R. Farquharson Sharp in the Everyman's Library series; Calder & Boyars Ltd for an extract from Eugène Ionesco's *The Killer,* in *Plays Volume III,* and an extract by Samuel Beckett in *International Theatre Annual No. I;* Faber & Faber Ltd for an extract reprinted from T. S. Eliot's *Four Quartets,* and with Grove Press, extracts, reprinted by permission from Samuel Beckett's *Waiting for Godot;* Granada Publishing Ltd for an extract by Peter Brook in *The Empty Space* published by MacGibbon & Kee Ltd; The Society of Authors on behalf of the Bernard Shaw Estate for an extract from George Bernard Shaw's *Man and Superman.*

Preface

A great many people derive a great deal of pleasure from reading plays. Would that pleasure be increased by an increase in their awareness of what they are doing? A script can be read casually, like a novel, mainly for the sake of the story, or it can be read, more like a code or a musical score, as a scenario for a series of theatrical impacts that can be achieved only in a public performance. Are we imagining actors moving on a stage or characters moving in a room? Do we even ask ourselves this question?

If you want to avoid self-consciousness about what you are doing when you read a script, do not read this book, which is written in the belief that the play comes more vividly to life in your mind if you are more aware of both similarities and differences between what the reader does and what actors do when looking at words on a two-dimensional page while thinking about three-dimensional action.

The well-trained actor has learned how to respond to a script not just intellectually and emotionally: he may feel physically involved in the tugs and rhythms of the action. The director reads a script with one eye on the problem of how the words can be fleshed into three-dimensional life. Not that the reader needs two or three years of training at a drama school before he can expect to get the most out of a script when he settles into his armchair, but he can, I believe, develop his talent for forming vivid impressions of theatrical action. The intention behind this book is to help.

How should we read stage directions? How can we imagine the theatrical impact of a sound effect? And of silence? What about the effect of colors, costumes, groupings, relative positions on the stage? Aren't characters sometimes saying something quite different from what their words are saying? What about the momentum an action can generate? Why is farce so much more amusing on the stage than on the page? These are some of the questions I try to answer in a book designed to contain as much practical help as I can give not just to the student and the specialist but to everyone for whom the word "theater" is not merely the name of the building they go to when they can afford to buy tickets.

Preface to the new edition

Reading one of your own books after an interval of twenty-one years is like reading a book by a stranger. I agree with most of what he said, and, in spite of feeling like an intruder, I'm glad for the opportunity to revise it, update it, and add a chapter about how to read a screenplay.

I don't think I've ever adequately expressed my gratitude to Geoffrey Strachan for being the leading man in its genesis. His company, Methuen, was publishing a lot of plays, and realizing that students of acting, students of drama, and other readers of scripts might like a guidebook to an area that had never been mapped, he commissioned me to write the book. After starting with a mixture of misgivings and enthusiasm, I was happy to find that in the United Kingdom the book was reprinted five times by the end of the 1980s, and in the United States it has been kept in print over twenty years.

While we were still working on the book, Geoffrey was promoted to the rank of managing director, and Nick Hern took over as editor. My thanks to them both, and to Grove-Atlantic for wanting to bring out a new edition.

I didn't
say it wuz! ! henjoyable readin.
I sd/ the guy had done some honest
work devilupping his theatre technique

———————————————

That don't necess/y mean making
reading matter @ all.

Ezra Pound
Letter to William Carlos Williams

I

The reader and the medium

What is a play?—The set and the atmosphere—The use of space—
The play as a series of impacts—Stage directions about action

What is a play?

We all think we know what a play is, but no one has ever suc-
ceeded in defining it. A novel or a poem is neither more nor less
than the words it consists of, but a script is obviously less than a
play, while a production is obviously more. So how do we lo-
cate its limits? Is it like a chemical substance that can never be
isolated, existing only in combination with other substances?

Reading a script can be all the more enjoyable if we remember that it wasn't intended for reading. We see words; we imagine sounds and pictures. When we go to the theater, we hear
words and sounds, but we see people and backgrounds; when
we read, we use our eyes on the element that is invisible in performance. During Shakespeare's lifetime, it was natural to talk
of *hearing* a play. "We'll hear a play tomorrow," promises Hamlet. "Will the King hear this piece of work?" Today, we always
talk of *seeing* a play, putting the emphasis on the action that is
visible.

When we read a play or a novel, we cannot take in more than
one impression at a time. As our eyes move laterally across the
printed lines, our brain receives each impact separately. The
information comes in a single jet, like water passing through a
narrow hole. In performance, several taps can be turned on at
the same time. Words, silences, sound effects, background
music, facial expressions, gestures, movements across the stage,
lighting, groupings, shadows, shapes and colors in the costume,
and decor—all these may be telling us something. At the same
time we are emotionally involved by the appearance, the voice,
the personality of the actors. We may feel in sympathy with one,
hostile to another. The words are all filtered to us through a

mesh. Our awareness of what they mean is inseparable from our awareness of vocal timbre, tone, timing, inflection, and atmosphere. In poetry and fiction, the basic currency is words; in drama it is the physical presence of the actors.

The set and the atmosphere

At a performance of Chekhov's *Three Sisters*, the storytelling starts with the stage picture, and we have picked up quite a lot of information before the first word is spoken. Here are the directions Chekhov gives:

> *The Prozorovs' house. A drawing room with columns beyond which a ballroom can be seen. Midday. Outside the sun is shining cheerfully. A table in the ballroom is being laid for lunch.*
> OLGA, *wearing the regulation dark blue dress of a high school teacher, carries on correcting her pupils' exercise books, standing up or walking about the room.* MASHA, *in a black dress, sits with her hat on her lap reading a book.* IRINA, *in a white dress, stands lost in thought.*

If these instructions have been followed, we will first form a composite impression, focusing gradually on the contrasts and details. At the same time as noticing the faces of the three women, we will observe the differences between them in dress, posture, and mood. Without noticing that our attention is being divided between them and the background, we will register the overall appearance of the room and the furniture, the midday sunlight outside, the ballroom visible behind the columns, the table being set in the hall. With only a few seconds to absorb all this before we start concentrating on the dialogue, we will form only a vague impression, which can be clarified as the scene proceeds. Our ears stay tuned to the words, while our eyes go on collecting details.

When we read the play, we run the risk of missing most of the atmosphere and the emotional impact that the scene can make. It's like reading a painter's description of his picture instead of looking at the canvas. We may read through the italicized stage direction as if it were a descriptive opening paragraph in a novel, or perhaps even more cursorily, feeling that the play doesn't properly begin until we get to the dialogue. If a novel started with a description, the writer could go on planting subsidiary clauses in his narrative to remind us of the information he had provided. If he used discreet phrases like "blinking in the brightness" or "staring unhappily into the dark corner," we wouldn't even feel that he was repeating himself. The playwright feels no need to provide reminders. He is assuming that the set, the lighting, the costumes, and the atmosphere that has been engendered will continuously support the words, like the orchestral accompaniment for a song.

What we can do when we are reading a play is make a conscious effort to digest the opening stage direction as if we were an architect considering a client's description of the house he wants us to design for him. He may only catalogue the relevant points: it is for us to form them carefully into a vivid mental picture that will stay with us throughout the ensuing dialogue.

The use of space

Many theater directors like to have a three-dimensional model of the set in front of them for at least some of the work they do in preparing a production. Without going to the lengths of building himself a model for each play, the reader can habituate himself to thinking of the action in relation to the writer's use of space. A novelist can move his narrative easily from battlefield to boudoir; so can the playwright, but without being able to shrink or expand the stage. He can ask for different areas to be used or lit, he can modulate between different ways of using them, but he does not enjoy the freedom of the novelist and the film director to zoom into an intimate close-up and then out into a wide-angle long shot.

From the black print on the two-dimensional page the reader of a play imaginatively builds himself a three-dimensional space in which figures are moving about. He may be visualizing actors on a stage or characters in a place. He may be pitching his mental pictures somewhere between the two possibilities, or, without noticing what he is doing, he may be shifting from one intermediate position to another. If he has seen the play in production he will be drawing intermittently on patchy memories. In any case the moving pictures in his mind's eye will sometimes be quite vivid, and sometimes quite dim. Sometimes they will fade altogether, leaving him aware only of words. At the moments when the play is coming to life in his imagination, his inner ear will be involved as actively as his inner eye. The voices and inflections he hears may belong either to the characters he is imagining or to the imaginary actors who are playing them. Again, he may be shuttling between the two possibilities, and again his imagination will be working better at some moments than others.

One of the advantages of envisaging actors on a stage (rather than characters in a room) is that you are more likely to remember the playwright's basic problem of filling the space at his disposal. A novelist could keep a character alone and motionless for twenty pages, provided that his stream of consciousness was rippling along interestingly. A play may contain many long speeches, but it is not likely to contain many long soliloquies, and whenever there is more than one character onstage, the reader needs to keep them all in mind. The temptation is to concentrate exclusively on whoever is speaking. A character who is listening—or not listening—may be contributing no less to the theatrical effect. In the Council Chamber scene in *Hamlet* (Act One, Scene Two), the Prince is silent but by no means unimportant during the first sixty-four lines of dialogue. He may be wearing black clothes that contrast with the sumptuous colors of the courtiers' costumes. He may be sitting at some distance from the King and Queen. In any case, his silence, his melancholy, and his detachment can make as much theatrical impact as any speeches Shakespeare could have written for him. The others are all hanging on the King's words, waiting for opportunities to curry favor by nodding agreement, murmuring approval, or laughing obsequiously at a joke. Hamlet's disaffection can make him into the most interesting character onstage.

This is an extreme case, but the good reader can hardly ever afford to forget any of the characters who are onstage. If they are not speaking, what are they doing?

The play as a series of impacts

Like a filmscript or a musical score, the script of a play is intended primarily for the use of professional performers. Unlike the novelist and the poet, the playwright has been counting on other people to mediate between his words and his public. But plays are usually much more enjoyable to read than filmscripts (in which the dialogue tends to matter less) and much more accessible than musical scores, though we do well to think of a text as a score for a series of theatrical impacts, many of which are not verbal. This encourages us to read more slowly, considering each new development in relation to the effect—or complex of effects—it could have on the audience. To receive the full impact of the dialogue, we need to imagine the sound of the spoken words and the edge they could have to cut against the other characters onstage. Often it's helpful to read the play aloud, sharing the dialogue with a friend. Read in this way, *Waiting for Godot* becomes funnier, livelier, and much more approachable.

Stage directions about action

Directions governing action need to be treated no less imaginatively than descriptions of sets. Reading the duel sequence in *Hamlet*, for instance, the eye is liable to glide quickly and ungratefully over such directions as *"They play," "The Queen falls,"* and *"Stabs the King."* The problem for the reader is partly visual, partly emotional. Apart from Attendant Lords and Ladies, there are six characters on stage: Hamlet, Horatio, the King and Queen, Laertes, and Osric. The movement revolves rapidly around the two traps that have been set to catch Hamlet's life: there is poison on one of the swords and poison that the King will put into a cup of wine. With the possible exception of Horatio, all six characters are moving about quite a lot from the moment the dueling starts. Three of them die within twenty-three lines and Hamlet twenty-seven lines later. The reader needs to have an impression of changes in position, in facial expression, in tone of voice. But the hardest element of all for him to imagine is the audience's emotional involvement in the physical action. The stage direction *"They play"* suggests nothing of the excitement that can be aroused by several minutes of grim dueling. Whatever the earlier provocation, Laertes has now put himself into the wrong by making himself a willing tool of the unscrupulous King. A noble prince is fighting against the accomplice of a murderer.

The direction *"Stabs the King"* calls for a much bigger imaginative effort. This is a crux of the tragedy. Hamlet is at last avenging the murder of his father and the seduction of his mother. At the same time he is striking a blow that cuts through all the other knots the plot has tied. Directly or indirectly, the King has caused the deaths of Polonius, Ophelia, Laertes, the Queen, and Hamlet himself. Even for the armchair reader the stage direction is satisfying, because it signals that justice is at last being done, but in performance the audience's longing for the villain to be punished has been strengthened by incomparably more powerful tugs of sympathy and hatred. The reader, alone with his book, should never forget how excited Victorian audiences could become, hissing the villain and cheering the valiant hero of a melodrama. *Hamlet* can be still more exciting. In any play the emotions that the writer is aiming to generate are largely dependent on a collective reaction, but the isolated individual can form a lively impression of them if he uses his imagination.

2

Sound effects

The quality of the sound—The buildup—The knocking on the castle gate—The knocking on the bedroom door

The quality of the sound

A sound effect presents the reader with the same difficulty as a visual effect: it is very hard to arrive at an accurate idea of its theatrical impact, or—if a rhythm is involved—of the accumulating pressure. The word "knocking" in italic print inside brackets does not tell us anything about the quality of the sound. How loud is it? How insistent? How impatient? How is the noise being made? An iron door knocker? A mailed fist thumping on a wooden door?

The buildup

As with stage directions like *"Stabs the King,"* the reader who is trying to imagine the theatrical impact of a sound effect must always consider it in the context of a developing momentum. Let's take an example.

The knocking on the castle gate

The knocking on the gate in *Macbeth* is both a minor climax in itself and part of the buildup toward a major climax—the discovery of the King's murdered body. In any context, loud and persistent knocking is unsettling for an audience, and in this murder scene it comes soon after the alarming sound of the bell. Both interruptions of the nocturnal silence occur when Macbeth is alone and in a jumpy state. As a soldier, he is used to killing but not to murder, and his first victim is to be his King.

The bell rings only once, but the sound reverberates ominously through the sleeping castle. Like all good *coups de théâtre,* the effect finds us at once prepared and unprepared. A servant

has been ordered to tell Lady Macbeth to strike upon the bell
when Macbeth's drink is ready, but since then, twenty-nine lines
of blank verse have put us off our guard. Frightened to find that
he cannot trust his own senses, Macbeth is clutching at an imaginary dagger, scaring himself (and us) with the nightmarish ideas
that are streaming through his brain. The howling of the wolf
is the "watch"—meaning either timepiece or watchman—that
alarms "withered Murder," which moves, like a ghost, "with
Tarquin's ravishing strides." Macbeth then commands the "sure
and firm-set earth" not to hear his footsteps "for fear/Thy very
stones prate of my whereabout." So, after starting with the in-
struction to the servant, the buildup to the sound effect is developed through these sinister references to unearthly noises.
Like any good buildup, it loads the context of expectation with
meaningful associations. The clang, when it comes, will give us
a jolt that is all the more disturbing if we connect it, half consciously, half unconsciously, not only with the sounds Macbeth
has mentioned but with the act of murder.

The triple rhyme bell/hell/knell, which tolls through his next
three lines, forges a theatrical link between the raucous noise and
the silent act of stabbing.

> I go, and it is done: the bell invites me.
> Hear it not, Duncan, for it is a knell
> That summons thee to heaven, or to hell.

The knocking does not start until the end of the following
scene, but the preparation for this climax has already begun.
Shakespeare has put our ears on the alert. Lady Macbeth, who
has been drinking, is buoyed up with daredevil euphoria, but
within two lines of her entrance she has checked herself to listen. There is no sound effect to represent the shrieking of the
owl, so she may either have heard it or imagined it, but her
metaphor "the fatal bellman/Which gives the stern'st goodnight"
connects the bird with both the bell and the murder. Macbeth
shouts "Who's there? What, ho?" from offstage. His first question, when he reappears with blood dripping from the daggers,
is whether she heard a noise. With his senses overstimulated,
he cannot differentiate between the real voices of the courtiers
he overheard praying and the imaginary voice that said "Macbeth
does murder sleep."

His fear makes her angry and the anger almost restores her
earlier confidence, though she may be trying to rally her own

spirits with the pun about *guilt* and *gilding* the faces of the grooms with blood to put the blame on them.

Immediately Macbeth is left on his own again, we hear loud knocking at the castle gate. Symbolism? A theatrical image to represent the pricking of his conscience? An exteriorization of his heartbeats? We are more likely to ask ourselves questions of this sort in reading, when (without even being aware that we have stopped) we can look up from the book to think. A performance gives us no means of controlling the rate at which new sensations are forced on us. With the physical impact of the knocking we are already being led toward the next climax, when the door will be opened. Who will come in?

Imagine a theater full of people unfamiliar with the play. More crucial than any symbolic overtone is the possibility that Macbeth and his wife will be exposed by the newcomer as murderers of their royal benefactor. There they are, with blood on their hands, still wearing yesterday's clothes. He is almost hysterical, she is under the influence of drink. Will they be sufficiently in control to cover their tracks? Why has someone arrived in the middle of the night? Or is it early morning already? Will he be able to guess whodunit? The spasmodic bursts of persistent knocking heighten the tension.

At first, left alone with the noise, Macbeth is as helpless and confused as he was during his vision of the dagger:

How is't with me, when every noise appals me?
What hands are here? ha! they pluck out mine eyes!
Will all great Neptune's ocean wash this blood
Clean from my hand? No; this my hand will rather
The multitudinous seas incarnadine,
Making the green one red.

He still can't distinguish the real noise from the noises inside his head, or the hand that is knocking from the fantasy hands trying to tear his eyes out. The drops of blood on his hand seem big enough to turn an ocean red. But the knocking reasserts the common-sense world of everyday reality, and when Lady Macbeth comes back, though she still talks in verse, her speech is objective, matter-of-fact. The knocking is "at the Southern entry" of the castle, and, without having heard his oceanic exaggeration, she optimistically contradicts it. "A little water clears us of this deed." But the man cannot snap so quickly back into the world of daylight facts.

Wake Duncan with thy knocking! I would thou couldst! Anyway, he goes with her to change into a nightgown, so the confrontation with the newcomer is postponed.

We move, instead, into a scene with a comic porter, while the knocking continues. If the noise is as enervating to the audience as it should be, it generates an almost tangible pressure on the Porter from every willpower in the auditorium. Why doesn't he open the door? How long is he going to go on grumbling? Theatrically, the straight line is the unfunniest distance between the two points. Between the intention and the action there is great scope for hesitation and digression. At the same time the noise and the enervation both help Shakespeare to equate the castle with hell:

> Here's a knocking indeed! If a man were porter of hell-gate, he should have old turning the key. (*knocking*) Knock, knock, knock! Who's there, i' th' name of Beelzebub?

Even when the Porter has opened the gate to admit Macduff and Lennox, the clowning goes on.

The action is moving inexorably toward the climax of discovering the dead King's bloody body, but in tragedy, as in a music-hall routine, a climax is more effective if the audience has been made to wait for it. No playwright was ever more expert than Shakespeare in gauging how long to protract a delay, and how much comedy to inject into a tragedy. There are drunken scenes or at least amusing allusions to drunkenness in nearly all the tragedies, and Macduff, who has no reason to suspect a murder, is still in a good enough humor, despite his long wait at the gate, to act as straight man for the Porter's clownish monologue about drink as a provoker of nose painting, lechery, and urine. And so we move on toward the next climax, when once again the bell will clang to sound the alarm that will rouse all the sleepers in the castle.

The knocking on the bedroom door

In Arthur Miller's play *Death of a Salesman*, Willy Loman's son Biff has been a schoolboy hero on the baseball field, but unsuccessful in adult life, except as a sexual freebooter. After building up some mystery about the reasons for his failure to settle down, the action has established that the turning point in his life occurred during his boyhood, when he went to see Willy in Boston. After that, he stopped trying, refused to make up the subject he had failed in his exam. Miller has whetted our curiosity about what happened in Boston, but he leaves us in suspense until he has prepared the context for showing why Willy feels responsible for the change that came over Biff. Evidence of the boy's kleptomania is provided before we flash back to the hotel bedroom, where Willy is with a woman, while the schoolboy Biff is outside, knocking at the door. We are not in suspense, this time, about the outcome, but additional pressure is generated by setting the flashback as an hallucination that occurs while Willy is in the cloakroom of a restaurant where his two sons are entertaining two girls. Miller swings us several times between present and past, introducing the knocking during one of the swings, and then bringing it back like a Wagnerian motif as we settle into the past for the showdown. The woman is laughing at Willy for his reluctance to open the door. He is too frightened even to shout "Go away." So the sound effect continues, uncomfortably, for some time before Willy lets Biff in:

WILLY: They're knocking on the wrong door.
THE WOMAN: But I felt the knocking. And he heard us talking in here. Maybe the hotel's on fire!
WILLY (*his terror rising*): It's a mistake.
THE WOMAN: Then tell him to go away!
WILLY: There's nobody there.
THE WOMAN: It's getting on my nerves, Willy. There's somebody standing out there and it's getting on my nerves!
WILLY (*pushing her away from him*): All right, stay in the bathroom here and don't come out. I think there's a law in Massachusetts about it, so don't come out. It may be that new room clerk. He looked very mean. So don't come out. It's a mistake, there's no fire.
(*The knocking is heard again . . .*)

With the woman in the bathroom, Willy could have got rid of Biff before she came out, but characteristically, after telling the boy to go downstairs and wait, Willy procrastinates. In his giggling admiration for Biff's skill in mimicking a schoolteacher, he encourages the boy to repeat the performance. When the woman starts laughing in the bathroom and emerges half naked, nothing Willy says or does can help. The experience is traumatic for Biff, and Willy has reason to feel guilty. As in *Macbeth,* the physical impact and the psychological resonance of the sound effect are inseparable.

3

Momentum and suspense

Beginnings—An argument in the street—The rhythm of progression —Rhythms in a play—Argument on a park bench— Maximum receptivity

The first question we ask of any play is "Does it come to life?" We don't mean "Is it lifelike?"; we mean "Is it alive?" We want it to seem like a growing organism, biologically independent of its creator. We want it to keep moving, but not like a machine that follows a set pattern. We want the movements to be unpredictable and interesting enough to keep our curiosity constantly whetted.

Beginnings

If the narrative flow of a novel is like a single jet of water, the story must start from a single point, and then there can be only one new impact at a time. The reader does not have to concentrate simultaneously on the background and the foreground; there will be one moment for the description of the pattern on the wallpaper, another for the girl's hair, another for what she says. The style of the writing is geared to the linear movements of the reading eye.

The playwright can simultaneously arouse the audience's curiosity in several areas. The silent action at the opening of *Three Sisters* makes us wonder why Olga is so restless. Why doesn't she sit down to correct the exercise books? Why is Masha reading with her hat on her lap? Is she about to get up and go? Will anyone be joining them at the table that is being prepared for lunch?

Unlike the novelist, who is addressing each reader separately —in private, as it were—the playwright must grab immediately at the corporate attention of his audience, implanting the same expectancy all over the auditorium. No hack writer of commercial thrillers has ever shown more skill than Shakespeare in arousing curiosity at the outset, hooking the audience's reactions along the same suspenseful track, scooping hundreds of consciousnesses into the same mood. *Hamlet* begins with a nervous sentry relieving another in front of a haunted castle, and within forty lines a ghost has appeared. *Macbeth* starts with thunder, lightning, and witches. At the opening of *Coriolanus* citizens are rioting with clubs and sticks.

A good opening provides an immediate spark of curiosity-whetting vitality, and with most scripts it is apparent quite early on whether the stuff we have in front of us would ignite theatrically. Not that the stage events need to be intrinsically sensational. As the curtain goes up on Oscar Wilde's *The Importance of Being Earnest,* a butler is arranging afternoon tea on a table and Algernon asks him whether he has cut the cucumber sandwiches for Lady Bracknell. At the start of *Death of a Salesman* Willy Loman is coming home, carrying his two sample cases, but something is wrong. His wife wasn't expecting him back so soon. Both beginnings give us something to look forward to: the arrival of Lady Bracknell; the solution of the minor mystery created by Willy's unexpected return.

During the fifties and sixties some beginnings went to the opposite extreme, as if to make it clear that no surprise packages would be unwrapped in the near future. In Beckett's *Waiting for Godot* the lights go up on two shabby men. One of them is trying to take one of his boots off. Harold Pinter's *The Birthday Party* starts with a woman in her sixties who is shouting through a hatch to tell her deckchair-attendant husband that his cornflakes are ready. At the beginning of Tom Stoppard's *Rosencrantz and Guildenstern Are Dead,* two bored attendant lords are whiling away the time by tossing coins.

But at least the playwright has put two characters in front of us. Something must happen. As with two animals in a cage at the zoo, we may not want to watch for very long, but the inclination, nearly always, is to wait until we have seen a sign of the interaction between them. Is anything interesting going to happen?

An argument in the street

Next time you go out of the house, your attention may be caught by an argument in the street. You may even stop to listen, wanting to see how the situation develops. It is potentially dramatic.

Even if it is an argument between two people speaking a language you do not understand, the tones of voice, the gestures, the pattern of the interaction may be highly watchable. Possibly the argument will culminate in a fight; possibly they will settle their differences and go off with their arms around each other's shoulders. Or it might peter out, or become boring, as it will if they go on making the same kind of point in the same tone of voice.

Perhaps you are a playwright watching the incident with a view to incorporating something similar into a new play. How will your script differ from your raw material? You are starting with realistic dialogue involving real conflict between real people: what do you have to do to make it dramatic? If you make a cassette recording of the argument on a machine hidden in your raincoat pocket, you will probably hear, when you play it back, moments of dialogue that are excitingly dramatic, even without the angry gestures and indignant expressions you remember having seen. But does the dialogue build theatrically toward a climax? And does that climax lead in the right way to the next?

What is the right way? Or if there are many ways, all equally right, how can we describe them?

The rhythm of progression

One of the main pleasures of poetry is the rhythm, which builds a pattern of expectations that will be partly fulfilled, partly frustrated. The frustrations will themselves be satisfying if the poet strikes an interesting balance between regularity and irregularity. Tennyson's poem "The Lady of Shalott" is boring both in its rhymes and in its rhythms, which hardly ever deviate from regular iambics: di-dum, di-dum, di-dum, di-dum.

> She left the web, she left the loom,
> She made three paces thro' the room,
> She saw the water-lily bloom,
> She saw the helmet and the plume . . .

Browning's poem "The Last Ride Together" is strongly rhythmic but more dramatic—less predictable and closer to the cadences of normal speech:

> Then we began to ride. My soul
> Smoothed itself out, a long-cramped scroll

Freshening and fluttering in the wind.
Past hopes already lay behind.
 What need to strive with a life awry?
Had I said that, had I done this,
So might I gain, so might I miss.
Might she have loved me? just as well
She might have hated,—who can tell?

Rhythms in a play

The rhythms in dramatic dialogue—whether it is in verse or in
prose—may be contributing greatly to the audience's pleasure
and to the buildup of its expectations, but the very fact that the
text is distributed between several speakers complicates the work-
ings of the rhythm, as in this passage from *As You Like It:*

> PHEBE: Good shepherd, tell this youth what 'tis to love.
> SILVIUS: It is to be all made of sighs and tears,
>   And so am I for Phebe.
> PHEBE: And I for Ganymede.
> ORLANDO: And I for Rosalind.
> ROSALIND: And I for no woman.

Other rhythms may be at work simultaneously. To the ex-
tent that each actor gives his character an individual tempo of
talking, reacting, thinking, moving, each one is different. As the
example from *Macbeth* showed us, the bursts of movement toward a climax can themselves constitute a rhythm, while sound
effects like knocking or visual effects like a revolving lighthouse
beam can introduce another rhythm, which is sustained either
briefly or through a prolonged sequence.

 The poignancy of the final moments in Chekhov's *The Cherry
Orchard* depends on combining different kinds of rhythm. The
house has been sold; the cherry orchard is going to be cut down.
After the sound effects that represent the family's departure—
doors being locked, carriages driving off—there is the first melancholy thud of an axe-edge hitting a tree. Then the sound of
dragging footsteps in the house that ought to be empty. The 87–
year-old manservant, Firs, appears in a jacket and white waist-
coat, with slippers on his feet. The feeble, faltering rhythm of
his final speech suggests that after he lies down he is never going
to get up again.

FIRS (*goes up to the door and touches the handle*): Locked. They've gone. (*Sits on the sofa.*) They forgot me. Never mind, I'll sit here a bit. And Mr. Leonid hasn't put his fur coat on, I'll be bound, he'll have gone off in his light one. (*Gives a worried sigh.*) I should have seen to it, these young folk have no sense. (*Mutters something which cannot be understood.*) Life's slipped by just as if I'd never lived at all. (*Lies down.*) I'll lie down a bit. You've got no strength left, got nothing left, nothing at all. You're just a—nincompoop. (*Lies motionless.*)

After this we get the final stage direction:

(*A distant sound is heard. It seems to come from the sky and is the sound of a breaking string. It dies away sadly. Silence follows, broken only by the thud of an axe striking a tree far away in the orchard.*)

Because of the distance, the sound is not loud, but the rhythm is merciless.

Argument on a park bench

In contrast to our imaginary argument in a street, let's consider the argument on the park bench in Edward Albee's play *The Zoo Story*. A placid, bespectacled middle-aged man, Peter, was reading his book on the bench until Jerry accosted him, apparently desperate for conversation.

JERRY: Now I'll let you in on what happened at the zoo: but first, I should tell you why I went to the zoo. I went to the zoo to find out more about the way people exist with animals, and the way animals exist with each other, and with people too. It probably wasn't a fair test, what with everyone separated by bars from everyone else, the animals for the most part from each other, and the people from the animals, but, if it's a zoo, that's the way it is. (*He pokes Peter on the arm.*) Move over.

PETER (*Friendly*): I'm sorry, haven't you enough room? (*He shifts a little.*)

JERRY (*Smiling slightly*): Well, all the animals are there, and all the people are there, and it's Sunday and all the children are there. (*He pokes Peter again.*) Move over.

PETER (*Patiently, still friendly*): All right. (*He moves some more, and Jerry has all the room he might need.*)

JERRY: And it's a hot day, so all the stench is there, too, and all the balloon sellers, and all the ice cream sellers, and all the seals are barking, and all the birds are screaming. (*Pokes Peter harder.*) Move over!

PETER (*Beginning to be annoyed*): Look here, you have more than enough room! (*But he moves more, and is now fairly cramped at one side of the bench.*)

JERRY: And I am there, and it's feeding time at the lion's house, and the lion keeper comes into the lion cage, one of the lion cages, to feed one of the lions. (*Punches Peter on the arm, hard.*) MOVE OVER!

PETER (*Very annoyed*): I can't move over any more, and stop hitting me. What's the matter with you?

JERRY: Do you want to hear the story? (*Punches Peter's arm again.*)

PETER (*Flabbergasted*): I'm not so sure! I certainly don't want to be punched in the arm.

JERRY (*Punches Peter's arm again*): Like that?

PETER: Stop it! What's the matter with you?

JERRY: I'm crazy, you bastard.

PETER: That isn't funny.

JERRY: Listen to me, Peter. I want this bench. You go sit on the bench over there, and if you're good I'll tell you the rest of the story.

The rhythm in the prose is neither regular nor strongly marked, but the pulse of the dialogue seems to be beating more feverishly as it moves toward a climax. Certain words are being repeated again and again—*zoo, animals, people, lion.* The blows on the arm are becoming harder and the demands more provocative. There is also a rhythm to the way Jerry keeps swinging between his description of the zoo and his demands for more space. Is he an animal caged by his own territorial imperative? Is he really crazy? The dialogue fans the flames of our curiosity about him. This is a highly dramatic sequence because the development is very rapid and we know it cannot go very much further in the same direction. Either there will be violence or a sudden cooling of the hostility, a climax or an anticlimax. As with a verse rhythm, expectations are being aroused that must either be fulfilled or satisfyingly frustrated. Given sufficient tension, an audience invariably makes half-conscious forecasts about how it will be resolved: to be wrong can be just as pleasurable as to be right. With *The Zoo Story* we are right to predict violence, and it is not altogether surprising when Jerry pulls out a knife, but it is surprising when he tosses it to Peter and when Peter lets himself be provoked into holding it out aggressively. It is more surprising still when Jerry impales himself on it.

Maximum receptivity

How can the reader put himself in a state of maximum receptivity to the multiple rhythms of a play? Theater directors need to be especially sensitive to the potentialities of a script, but it is almost as hard for them to envisage a production as it is for a conductor to sit down with an orchestral score and imagine the work in performance. I know one theater director who never settles down to a new script without having a bath, shaving, and putting on a clean shirt, just as if he were going out to the theater. He takes the telephone off the hook before sitting down in his favorite armchair, and he doesn't get up till he has finished the first act, when he allows himself fifteen minutes before starting on the second.

If a script is a score for a series of impacts, it is important to approximate as closely as you can to receiving them uninterruptedly in the order the playwright arranged them and within the same span of time. A play is hardly ever too long to read at a single sitting, and with any work, new or old, the ideal reader will try to clear his mind of all expectations except those which accumulate as he reads. Each impact will then come as a surprise and each surprise should be considered three-dimensionally. How is it filling the space between the actors and the audience?

Reading like this, you are more alert to the play's rhythms, even if you are not thinking about them in terms of rhythm.

4

Not by words alone

The silence under the words—The conjurer's patter—Visual trans-
formation—The shuffling footsteps—Visual inequalities

The silence under the words

In 1962, making one of his rare speeches, Harold Pinter said:

> There are two silences. One when no word is spoken. The
> other when perhaps a torrent of language is being employed.
> This speech is speaking of a language locked beneath it. That
> is its continual reference. The speech we hear is an indica-
> tion of that we don't hear. It is a necessary avoidance, a vio-
> lent, sly, anguished or mocking smokescreen which keeps the
> other in its place. When true silence falls we are still left with
> echo but are nearer nakedness. One way of looking at speech
> is to say it is a constant stratagem to cover nakedness.

Sometimes it is relatively easy for the armchair reader to
unlock the language beneath the dialogue. In the final act of *The
Cherry Orchard* the family is about to move out of the old house,
which has been bought by the businessman Lopakhin. There is
a sequence between him and Madam Ranevsky's adopted daughter, Varya, who has been working more or less as a housekeeper.
She could look after the house for him if he marries her, as,
apparently, he wants to. Alone with Madam Ranevsky, he says:

> If it's not too late I don't mind going ahead even now. Let's
> get it over and done with. I don't feel I'll ever propose to her
> without you here.

But this is what happens when he is eventually left alone with
Varya:

> VARYA (*spends a long time examining the luggage*): That's funny,
>   I can't find it anywhere.

LOPAKHIN: What are you looking for?

VARYA: I packed it myself and I still can't remember. (*Pause.*)

LOPAKHIN: Where are you going now, Varya?

VARYA: Me? To the Ragulins'. I've arranged to look after their place, a sort of housekeeper's job.

LOPAKHIN: That's in Yashnevo, isn't it? It must be fifty odd miles from here. (*Pause.*) So life has ended in this house.

VARYA (*examining the luggage*): Oh, where can it be? Or could I have put it in the trunk? Yes, life has gone out of this house. And it will never come back.

LOPAKHIN: Well, I'm just off to Kharkov. By the next train. I have plenty to do there. And I'm leaving Yepikhodov in charge here, I've taken him on.

VARYA: Oh, have you?

LOPAKHIN: This time last year we already had snow, remember? But now it's calm and sunny. It's a bit cold though. Three degrees of frost, I should say.

VARYA: I haven't looked. (*Pause.*) Besides, our thermometer's broken. (*Pause.*)

A voice at the outer door: MR. LOPAKHIN!

LOPAKHIN: (*as if he had long been expecting this summons*): I'm just coming. (*Goes out quickly.*)

At the beginning of this sequence the girl's embarrassment increases when he fails to speak first. She knows that he knows why she has come into the room, but she still feels compelled to improvise a pretext for being there. The pretense of looking for something among the luggage also gives her an excuse for turning her back on him. Had she been bold enough to look him in the eye and wait for him to speak first, the outcome might have been quite different. He is obviously in two minds about whether he wants her as his wife, and when he inquires about her plans, he may, clumsily and halfheartedly, be leading up to asking her to stay—or he may be uncertain of where he wants to take the conversation. The moment for the crucial question is then allowed to slip by. This cannot accurately be described as either intentional or unintentional. He is not fully in control either of himself or the situation.

Lopakhin's remark about the distance of Yashnevo is just a piece of procrastination, and, after an agonized pause, he is out of his depth and treading water when he says that life in the house has come to an end. His embarrassment exacerbates hers.

There is irony in his being able to ask Yepikhodov to stay while he is unable to ask her, but he is reduced to talking about the weather. It is an enormous relief for him when the shout from the yard provides a pretext for leaving the room. There is not a single direct expression of emotion in the sequence, but the audience can gauge what is going on underneath the surface of irrelevant words.

The conjurer's patter

Most conjuring tricks could be performed in silence, but they would be much less theatrical. Without relying entirely on his patter to distract the spectators from what he is doing with his hands, the performer is capitalizing on the fact that their attention is divided. So is the playwright. A good script is incomparably more impressive and interesting than the text of a conjurer's patter, which would be very boring to read, though there may be an ironic contrast between what is being said and what is being done.

In Strindberg's play *The Father*, the mother is trying to drive her husband mad by encouraging his doubts about the paternity of the child, Bertha. He is enraged to the point of threatening that he will kill her, but in the end his old nurse soothes him into letting go of the revolver. She then coaxes his arms into a straitjacket.

NURSE (*enters*): Mr. Adolf, what is it?
CAPTAIN (*looks at the revolver*): Have you taken the cartridges?
NURSE: Yes, I've hidden them away. But sit down and calm yourself, and I'll bring them back to you.
    She takes the CAPTAIN *by the arm and coaxes him down into the chair, where he remains sitting dully. Then she takes the straitjacket and goes behind his chair,* BERTHA *tiptoes out left.*
NURSE: Do you remember, Mr. Adolf, when you were my dear little baby, how I used to tuck you up at night and say your prayers with you? And do you remember how I used to get up in the night to fetch you a drink? Do you remember how I lit the candle and told you pretty stories when you had bad dreams and couldn't sleep? Do you remember?
CAPTAIN: Go on talking, Margaret. It soothes my head so. Go on talking.

NURSE: All right, but you must listen, then. Do you remember how once you took the big carving knife and wanted
to make boats, and how I came in and had to get the knife
away from you by telling you a story? You were such a silly
baby, so we had to tell you stories, because you thought
we all wanted to hurt you. Give me that snake, I said,
otherwise he'll bite you. And you let go of the knife. (*Takes
the gun from the* CAPTAIN'S *hand.*) And then, when you had
to get dressed and you didn't want to. Then I had to coax
you and say I'd give you a gold coat and dress you like a
prince. And I took your little body-garment, which was
only of green wool, and held it in front of you and said:
"Put your arms in," and then I said: "Sit still, now, and be
a good boy while I button up the back!" (*She has got the
straitjacket on him.*) And then I said: "Stand up now, and
walk nicely, so I can see how you look." (*She leads him to
the sofa.*) And then I said: "Now it's time to go to bed."
CAPTAIN: What's that, Nanny? Must I go to bed when I'm
dressed? Damnation! What have you done to me? (*Tries
to free himself.*) Oh, you damned cunning woman! Who
would have believed you were so crafty? (*Lies down on the
sofa.*) Caught, cropped, and cozened! And not to be allowed to die!

The scene works on several levels for both the audience in
the theater and the reader. We don't want Bertha to be shot, so
there is a thrillerlike suspense until the revolver is safely out of
the Captain's hand. Underneath this action is a Strindbergian
irony that cannot be fully effective for the reader unless he is
visualizing the characters in action, using his imagination to
create a performance for himself.

The appearance of the old nurse is reassuring: her voice and
her presence carry associations of the child's protected existence
in the nursery, the room where help is always available and nothing worse can happen than a bump on the head. But the straitjacket in the old woman's hand warns us contrapuntally that her
former nursling is in danger. What she says is soothing like a
lullaby; what she does is unmanning like a castration. Her action reduces the Captain to the defenseless feebleness of the child
he was in the nursery. There is double irony—and double bluff—
in her reminiscence about having to trick him when he didn't
believe they meant well by him. She is tricking him now, but he

catches on too late to the contradiction in what she is saying. The speech is calculated to divert attention from what the hands are doing, but the words are also ramming home Strindberg's point that throughout his life the man has been a victim of superior female cunning. The reader can imagine the cosy, comfortable timbre of the old woman's voice, with its coaxing inflections, while picturing what she is doing to reduce a dangerous-looking male with a revolver into ridiculous-looking helplessness, his arms secured behind his back like a lunatic.

In these sequences from *The Cherry Orchard* and *The Father* there is a wide gap between spoken words and the feeling or purpose underlying them, but in neither passage is it difficult for the actor or for the reader to be sure of how the words ought to be spoken. Like most politicians, the characters are using language not to reveal but to conceal their intentions. We know what Lopakhin, Varya, and the Nurse are up to. We also know that all three would talk quite differently if they were saying what they meant. The irony is visible in the wide space between language and intention, though none of the three characters is conscious of what the playwright is saying.

Visual transformation

There can be many different kinds of gaps between what is being said and what is being done. In Scene Twelve of Brecht's play *The Life of Galileo,* there is nothing in the dialogue and precious little in the stage directions to tell the reader that a change of costume is producing a change of theatrical identity, which effectively amounts to change of personality. Forbidden by the Inquisition to publish his evidence for believing that the earth is not the center of the universe, Galileo remains silent for eight years. His best friend inside the church has been Cardinal Barberini, a mathematician, sophisticated and tolerant. When he becomes Pope Urban VIII, there seems to be a genuine prospect of ecclesiastical enlightenment. In Scene Twelve we see him giving audience to the Cardinal Inquisitor, who is arguing that the new cosmological ideas constitute a serious threat to the Church's authority. The scene opens with three loud shouts of "No" from the Pope, but while he is being dressed by acolytes in his papal regalia, the Inquisitor does most of the talking. The vestments and papal crown seem to add their weight to the few words that the new Pope utters. After the change of costume is

complete, he gives permission for his former friend to be threatened with torture. They may show him the instruments. "That
will suffice, your Holiness," says the Inquisitor. "Signor Galileo
is an expert on instruments."

However appreciatively the reader responds to verbal points
like this one, he is liable to miss the main theatrical point. The
stage direction at the beginning of the scene is casually terse:

> *An apartment in the Vatican. Pope* URBAN VIII, *formerly Cardinal
> Barberini, has received the* CARDINAL INQUISITOR. *During the au-
> dience he is being robed. Outside is the sound of many shuffling feet.*

Before the last two speeches in the scene there is one more stage
direction:

> *Pause. The* POPE *is now in his full robes.*

The reader is given no other reminder of what the audience has
been watching all through the scene. The Inquisitor will have
moved very little, the Pope not at all, but the sumptuous vestments have been reverently handed by acolytes to the senior
acolyte, who has reverently been draping them around the man
who was wearing ordinary clothes. The transformation is a spectacular one, and though Barberini's face does not change, the
effect is almost as if he were putting on a mask. The costume is
changing him into a pope. The individual is disappearing into
the office. It is Galileo's friend who holds out against the Inquisitor; it is the Pope who submits.

The shuffling footsteps

At the end of the opening stage direction is another sentence
that the reader is liable to credit with very much less than its full
theatrical value. The shuffling, which goes on throughout the
conversation, has an enervating effect on the Pope, which will
probably be registered only very casually by the actor. Perhaps
an irritated movement of the head; perhaps a hint of tension in
the voice. Almost nothing is said about the noise until just before the decision that forms the climax of the scene, when, knowing he is on the point of capitulating to orthodox opinion, the
Pope shows his anger, but disguises it, as if the people in the
corridor were the only cause. "This tramping in the corridors is
intolerable. Is the whole world coming here?" "Not the whole

world," answers the Cardinal Inquisitor, "but its best part." This is apt because the sound has served to reinforce the first question that the Inquisitor put:

> Your Holiness, there are assembled here doctors of all faculties, representatives of all the holy orders and of the whole priesthood who have come, with their childlike faith in the Word of God as revealed in the Scriptures, to receive from your Holiness the confirmation of their faith. Will your Holiness now tell them that the Scriptures can no longer be regarded as true?

These are the strongest sheep in the flock, which the shepherd has to consider before answering the question that finally becomes crucial in the discussion. After eight years, Galileo has been allowed to publish his book on condition that the last word is not with science but with faith. The condition has been fulfilled by ending with a dialogue between a stupid man, who believes the sun goes around the earth, and a clever man, who contradicts him. Galileo has contrived to give the last word to the stupid man. In performance, the footsteps unsettle the audience, while they unsettle the Pope with their reminder that the cleverest men in the Church are being unsettled by doubts that Galileo is fomenting.

The writing in this scene is very densely textured. Though the bulk of the argument comes from a viewpoint Brecht dislikes, he lets the Inquisitor make out a very good case. Out of respect for the Pope, he has to choose his phrases carefully, but his logic is intricate and forceful. The reader may need to go through the passage twice—once for the argument and once for the succession of theatrical moments in which the gradual change of costume and the continuous sound effect combine to push the character away from the determination he shows at the beginning of the sequence, exerting considerable vocal energy to say "No." As the ceremony of robing proceeds, his stature is visibly enhanced. In other words, his visual dominance in the discussion is being asserted more and more strongly, but he still has to end up saying "Yes."

Visual inequalities

Reading a play, our natural tendency is to assume that a character's power depends on his words. If there is nothing to contradict the assumption, we would take it that the one with the most to say is dominant. There is nothing in the text to remind us that in performance, costume, movement, and relative positions onstage can enable one character to secure more of the audience's attention than another.

Like the park bench in *The Zoo Story,* the whole stage may be made to seem like a battlefield in which one territorially acquisitive character is competing with another, not for ownership of the space but for ascendancy. Or it may be, as in the duel scene from *Hamlet,* that the action brings first one character, then another, into prominence. The chairs of state on which the King and Queen sit may be on a rostrum and will certainly be in a commanding position. Their costumes confirm their priority in rank, and from the moment of putting Laertes's hand into Hamlet's (Act Five, Scene Two, line 224), the King has established himself as the man who is presiding over the sport. Osric judges the bout and at moments of appeal (e.g., lines 278–9) he is in the center of focus.

An audience generally tends to focus its attention on whoever is moving or, when there is no movement, on the upstage figure in a group. In a sequence like this one, with a great deal of movement, the focus shifts constantly. Knowing that one of the foils is poisoned, we watch Laertes very carefully when, pretending the one he has taken is too heavy for him, he selects another (line 262). During the dueling, our concentration is likely to be divided equally between him and Hamlet. The first time they break off, it is again the King who claims our attention, when he pops what he says is a pearl into the wine (line 280); the second interruption centers on the Queen, when, after giving Hamlet her napkin to wipe his brow, she drinks from the poisoned cup. The third bout of swordplay brings our attention back to the duelists and momentarily to Osric when he pronounces judgment. The focus then shifts very rapidly from Laertes, who wounds Hamlet when he is off his guard, to Hamlet, who fights furiously for possession of the poisoned foil, and then to the Queen, who falls to the ground.

Hamlet now takes charge of the situation, ordering the doors to be locked. Laertes becomes the center of attention again when he confesses the truth in an eight-line speech, which culminates in a denunciation of the King. Hamlet then dominates again, stabbing the King and forcing him to drink the poisoned wine. Laertes brings himself back briefly into prominence with his dying speech, but the focus is then on Hamlet until his own death. Horatio is very much the subordinate character, except briefly, when he tries to drink from the poisoned cup.

Domination of a scene does not depend on dominating the other characters: the feeblest of victims may win the lion's share of the audience's attention, and a dying speech is nearly always a big theatrical moment. In the sequence we took from *The Father*, the power shifts from the dangerous-seeming man to the harmless-seeming old woman, but their share of the audience's attention is more or less equal throughout. At the beginning of the sequence from *Galileo*, the Cardinal Inquisitor's costume gives him visual superiority, although Barberini has already been proclaimed Pope. As we saw, the change of costume makes him outshine the Cardinal Inquisitor but, ironically, the more powerful he looks, the less power he has to assert his personal willpower.

5

Costume and identity

*A quick transformation—Dual identities—Disguise—Confusion
without disguise—The prostitute and her cousin*

A quick transformation

The *Galileo* sequence provides a slow-motion sample of a kind of transformation that is frequent in drama and a rare in cinema. Often it involves disguise. In the last act of Shakespeare's *Measure for Measure* there is a superb climax when the Duke, who has been disguised as a friar, averts a miscarriage of justice. He reveals his identity by exposing the colorful, opulent, aristocratic costume under the drab habit that he discards. As with the Cardinal in *Galileo*, the face remains the same but, theatrically, the identity changes. A feeble-seeming man, who was about to be led off to prison, is suddenly the most authoritative figure in the stage picture. The corruptible Deputy, Angelo, who seemed to have been in sole control of Vienna, has all the time been under the godlike supervision of the disguised Duke.

Lucio has revealed himself as an opportunist who shifts his loyalties quickly and cynically. He has gossiped with the Friar about the absent Duke, whom he described as "a very superficial, ignorant, unweighing fellow" (Act Three, Scene Two, line 135). Later, in the presence of Angelo, he denounces the Friar as if he had been the one to slander the absent ruler.

LUCIO: 'Tis he, my lord . . . Come hither, goodman baldpate. Do you know me?
DUKE: I remember you, sir, by the sound of your voice. I met you at the prison, in the absence of the duke.
LUCIO: Oh, did you so? And do you remember what you said of the duke?
DUKE: Most notedly, sir.

LUCIO: Do you so, sir? And was the duke a flesh-monger, a
fool, and a coward, as you then reported him to be?

Angelo orders the Provost to arrest the Friar, who resists, claim-
ing to love the Duke as well as himself. When Angelo tells Lucio
to help the Provost, he plucks at the Friar's hood:

LUCIO: Come sir, come sir, come sir: foh sir, why you bald-
pated lying rascal . . . you must be hooded, must you? Show
your knave's visage, with a pox to you . . . show your sheep-
biting face, and be hanged an hour . . . Will't not off?

The Friar's identity has been no secret from the audience, who
could not otherwise have enjoyed the irony in what he says about
loving the Duke. Sooner or later the disguise was bound to be
discarded, but it is clever to trigger the revelation through the
initiatives of the two men who will be discomfited most. As
the reader can imagine, the sudden blaze of rich colors from the
Duke's costume is like the sun of justice coming out from behind
a cloud. The stage picture quickly reorients itself. Angelo, who
had been giving all the orders, is eclipsed; Lucio will be punished
for his duplicity and Shakespeare celebrates with a joke:

DUKE: Thou art the first knave that e'er mad'st a duke.

Dual identities

Earlier in the play, when the Duke goes into disguise, Shakespeare
is, in effect, loading him with a dual identity. For most of the
time that he is dressed like a friar, he talks and behaves like a
friar. Knowing that he is not a friar, the audience has the satis-
faction of being aware of the distance between the Duke's "real"
character and the role he is playing. It is a case of play-acting
inside a play. Similarly, in *King Lear*, Edgar effectively becomes
two people—a young nobleman and a half-crazy beggar—while
Kent is both an earl and a servant.

In performance, confusions of identity can be extremely entertaining, and moments of recognition or revelation extremely
satisfying, but for the armchair reader, whose contact with the
action is not through the physical presence of the actors but
through words, it may be hard to understand why so many plays
revolve around problems of identity. Why do conventional plots

contain so many identical twins, so many babies swapped while still in their cradles, so many men disguised as women and women disguised as men, so many characters who find themselves putting on elaborate performances in response to other people's determination to behave toward them as if they were someone else? Common in opera, these plot devices are all rare in film and television drama.

The central character in Gogol's comedy *The Government Inspector* is not a government inspector but a clerk without even enough money to pay his bill at the hotel. Hearing that the landlord is going to complain to the Mayor about him, he threatens to complain about the landlord. A moment later his servant Ossip comes in.

OSSIP: Here—the Mayor's downstairs . . . asking all sorts of questions about you.

KHLESTIAKOV (*terrified*): What? No! That damned landlord's complained already! Suppose he's come to take me to prison . . . ? Well, what of it, they'd have to treat me like a gentleman, and at least there'd be food . . . No! No! I won't go, someone might see me, one of those officers or that pretty little daughter of the seed merchant I've been flirting with, I can't let them all see me being dragged off to prison. Who the devil does he think he is, anyway, this landlord? I'm not some miserable shopkeeper or smelly laborer! (*Screwing up his courage.*) I'll tell him to his face. "How dare you!" I'll say. "Who do you think you are?" I'll say. "Who the hell are you . . . ?"

The doorhandle turns, and KHLESTIAKOV *grows pale and shrinks into himself. Enter the* MAYOR, *shutting the door on* DOBCHINSKY. KHLESTIAKOV *and the* MAYOR, *both equally terrified, stare at each other in silence for some moments. The* MAYOR *recovers first and comes to attention.*

MAYOR: May I take the liberty of wishing you good-day, sir?

KHLESTIAKOV (*bowing*): Much obleeged, I'm sure.

MAYOR: I hope you'll pardon the intrusion . . .

KHLESTIAKOV: Not at all.

MAYOR: It's my duty, as senior official in the town, to see that all visitors and persons of rank and quality suffer no inconvenience . . .

KHLESTIAKOV (*breaks in, stammering, but raising his voice as he goes on*): B-b-b-but what could I d-d-d-do ... I'm g-g-going to p-p-pay, I really am, they're sending money from home ...

   Enter DOBCHINSKY, *shutting the door on* BOBCHINSKY. It's his fault, not mine. The food's uneatable, terrible, the meat's like shoe leather and the soup, God only knows what he puts in the soup. I had to throw some out the window just now. That man's starving me! And the tea ... you'd never know it was tea, it stinks like fish-glue! Why should I ... why ... I don't see why ...

MAYOR (*intimidated*): Please forgive me, it's really not my fault. The meat in the market's always good, I see to that, it's all brought in by good honest dealers, we've never had a complaint like this before. I really can't imagine where he could get bad meat. But sir, if you aren't satisfied with things here, I'd best escort you to other quarters ...

KHLESTIAKOV: No, no, no! I know what you mean with your "other quarters"—you mean the jail. Well, I won't go! You've got no right, how dare you! I-I-I'm a Government official from Petersburg, I-I-I ...

MAYOR (*aside*): Dear God, he's furious! Those damned shop-keepers have told him everything.

KHLESTIAKOV (*wildly bluffing*): You can bring a whole regiment with you, I still won't go! I'll write straight to the Minister, I will! (*He thumps the table.*) Who do you think you are? You ... You ...!

MAYOR (*trembling, stands to attention*): Oh, please, sir, have pity on us, don't ruin us! My wife ... my little children ... it'll ruin us!

Like the other corrupt officials in the town, the Mayor lives in fear of being found out. Khlestiakov is under no misapprehension about his identity—only about his motive for coming to the room—but the Mayor is confused about Khlestiakov's identity. The comedy has nothing to do with verbal wit, and the reader's enjoyment must depend partly on how vividly he can imagine the physical details—the appearance of the two men, their changing expressions, their attempts to look and sound less nervous than they actually are.

Disguise

It is even harder for the reader to envisage the theatrical effect when characters are disguising their "real" personality, not by putting on a brave face (like Khlestiakov and the Mayor), but dressing up (like Shakespeare's Duke). It is not only in tragedy that Shakespeare uses disguise to create dual identity. He makes frequent use of the device in comedy and he is sometimes very perfunctory about the reasons he gives his characters for assuming a false identity: in *Twelfth Night* Viola has no convincing motivation for dressing up as a boy.

The convention that stage disguises are impenetrable is sometimes troublesome to modern audiences. How can King Lear be stupid enough not to notice that his servant Caius is actually the Earl of Kent, who is supposed to be in exile? If Orlando in *As You Like It* really loves Rosalind, how can he possibly fail to recognize her when she is standing next to him, even if she is dressed as a boy? The reader is at an advantage in not having to watch the characters looking at each other, but at a disadvantage in not being able to catch the full flavor of jokes that depend on physical appearance or the full theatricality of recognitions, where the characters may be reacting differently to the revelation.

The Greek dramatist Menander, who wrote in the third century B.C., was the first playwright to make a thorough exploration of how confusion over identity could be exploited. One of Plutarch's anecdotes about him drives home the point that in this kind of play the words are of secondary importance. A few days before a Dionysian festival, one of Menander's friends was concerned that his play was still not finished. "Yes it is," said the playwright. "I've done the plot. Now all I have to do is write the lines." To the reader, the lines constitute the play: a mere synopsis of the plot is indigestible and extremely boring. But in Menander's plays the words are only trimmings around the structural confusions of identity. The plots contain the germs of countless subsequent farces, comedies, thrillers, films, and television dramas. Children have been brought up in ignorance of their parentage; brothers unwittingly flirt with their sisters; husbands make love to their disguised wives in the belief that they are embarking on an exciting adultery; nubile ladies reject eligible bachelors, believing them to be philandering husbands.

Confusion without disguise

The confusion of identity does not need to be based on disguise. Oliver Goldsmith's comedy *She Stoops to Conquer* introduces a rich hero, Young Marlow, who is shy with girls of his own class but feels quite at ease with barmaids. Confronted with the desirable Kate Hardcastle, he is gauche to the point of speechlessness, but a practical joke, played by her boorish half brother, Tony Lumpkin, convinces Marlow and his friend Hastings that they are in an inn when actually they are in the Hardcastles' house. The confusion involves not only identity but manners. The behavior appropriate to the paying guest at an inn is not appropriate to the suitor invited to the house of his future father-in-law:

MARLOW (*After drinking*): And you have an argument in your cup, old gentleman, better than any in Westminster Hall.
HARDCASTLE: Ay, young gentleman, that, and a little philosophy.
MARLOW (*Aside*): Well, this is the first time I ever heard of an innkeeper's philosophy.
HASTINGS: Let's see your list of the larder, then. I ask it as a favor. I always match my appetite to my bill of fare.
MARLOW (*To* HARDCASTLE, *who looks at them with surprise*): Sir, he's very right, and it's my way, too.
HARDCASTLE: Sir, you have a right to command here. Here, Roger, bring us the bill of fare for tonight's supper. I believe it's drawn out. Your manner, Mr. Hastings, puts me in mind of my uncle, Colonel Wallop. It was a saying of his, that no man was sure of his supper till he had eaten it.
HASTINGS (*Aside*): All upon the high rope! His uncle a colonel! We shall soon hear of his mother being a justice of peace.

They go on, patronizingly, to tell him what they want for their supper. Later, taking Kate for a maidservant, Marlow tries to flirt with her, succeeding, almost accidentally, in winning her love.

The amorous entanglements in Menander's plots often involve a courtesan or a slave who will subsequently be recognized—probably through a birthmark—as wellborn and therefore marriageable. There have been variations on this theme in plots that give aristocratic heroes different reasons for wooing a girl while in the guise of a low-ranking soldier (as in Sheridan's *The Rivals*) or a humble and penniless student (as in Beaumarchais's *The Barber of Seville*).

Oscar Wilde's sophisticated plotting in *The Importance of Being Earnest* culminates in a characteristically Menandrian revelation: the hero has a noble pedigree, so no one can object to the marriage. At the beginning, when Lady Bracknell interviewed Jack Worthing as a candidate for the hand of her daughter Gwendolen, he could say nothing about his parentage except that he was found in a large black leather handbag with handles, which was erroneously given to Mr. Thomas Cardew in the cloakroom of Victoria Station, when he was on his way to the seaside resort that provided the infant with a surname. Lady Bracknell's main function in the play is to represent the social order that rejects foundlings as unacceptable marriage partners. When it emerges that the handbag contained the infant son of her own sister, she is satisfied.

The other main source of comedy in the play is a different kind of identity-confusion. Jack has been going under the alias of Ernest Worthing when he was in the country, and Gwendolen has declared that she would be unable to love a man with any other Christian name. Cecily Cardew arrives at the same decision after Jack's friend, Algernon Moncrieff (who will turn out to be his younger brother) has introduced himself to her under the same alias, pretending to be Jack's younger brother, Ernest. Cecily and Algernon withdraw into the house together just before Jack arrives in mourning to announce Ernest's death, and when Gwendolen appears, it looks as though both girls are engaged to the same Ernest. Meanwhile both men have arranged with the local clergyman to be christened Ernest, but when Jack comes into the garden, Cecily reveals his identity, and when Algy appears, Gwendolen, his cousin, reveals his. After the denouement has brought the revelation that Jack is Lady Bracknell's nephew, his name turns out to be Ernest John.

The prostitute and her cousin

Brecht's use of disguise in *The Good Person of Szechwan* could be seen as an anti-Romantic and Marxist inversion of the disguise convention as used in *Twelfth Night* and *As You Like It*. Brecht's prostitute heroine, Shen Teh, appears in a mask and male clothes to sort out the financial troubles that her generosity has caused her. Rewarded by three itinerant gods for the hospitality she has given them, she has been exploited by people who find how easy it is to take advantage of her new affluence. She hasn't the heart to evict the homeless family of eight that comes to camp in her tobacconist's shop, and she is equally at the mercy of the greedy and the needy—landlady, carpenter, tradesmen. To save herself from losing all her money, she resorts to the old comedy stratagem of inventing a relation—a cousin who is a rich and respectable businessman, Shui Ta. He behaves toughly toward those who have exploited her inability to say "No" and he arranges a marriage for her with a rich barber, Shu Fu.

It is characteristic of Brecht's ironies that later on, when Shen Teh (wearing her own clothes) strikes up a relationship with Yang Sun, who wants to be a pilot, his interest in her turns out to be more financially than romantically motivated. The scene in which she discovers this—while disguised as Shui Ta—depends for its effect on the old theatrical device of identity-confusion. As in the Forest of Arden sequences between Rosalind and Orlando, the boy fails to realize that he is not only talking *about* his girl, but *to* her. Shen Teh is willing to sell her shop for three hundred silver dollars, which Yang Sun needs to bribe his way into a job as a pilot. He has promised to marry her, but he does not intend to take her with him to Pekin.

SHUI TA: It costs quite a bit for two.

SUN: Two? I'm leaving the girl here. She'd only be a liability at first.

SHUI TA: I see.

SUN: Why do you look at me as if I was something the cat had brought in? Beggars can't be choosers.

SHUI TA: And what is my cousin to live on?

SUN: Can't you do something for her?

SHUI TA: I will look into it. (*Pause.*) I should like you to hand me back the two hundred silver dollars, Mr. Yang Sun, and leave them with me until you are in a position to show me two tickets to Pekin.

SUN: My dear cousin, I should like you to mind your own business.

SHUI TA: Miss Shen Teh . . .

SUN: You just leave her to me.

SHUI TA: . . . may not wish to proceed with the sale of her business when she hears . . .

SUN: Oh yes she will.

SHUI TA: And you are not afraid of what I may have to say against it?

SUN: My dear man!

SHUI TA: You seem to forget that she is flesh and blood, and has a mind of her own.

SUN (*Amused*): It astounds me what people imagine about their female relations and the effect of sensible argument. Haven't they ever told you about the power of love, the twitching of the flesh? You want to appeal to her reason? She hasn't any reason! All she's had is a lifetime of ill treatment, poor thing! If I put my hand on her shoulder and say "You're coming with me," she'll hear bells and not recognize her own mother.

SHUI TA (*Laboriously*): Mr. Yang Sun!

SUN: Mr. . . . whatever your name is!

SHUI TA: My cousin is indebted to you because . . .

SUN: Let's say because I've got my hand inside her blouse? Stuff that in your pipe and smoke it! (*He takes another cigar, then sticks a few in his pocket, and finally puts the box under his arm.*) You're not to go to her empty-handed: we're getting married, and that's settled. And she'll bring the three hundred with her or else you will: either her or you. (*Exit.*)

This dialogue relies on the rudimentary dramatic irony of letting the audience into the secret (which is being kept from Yang Sun) about the identity of the "man" he is talking to. As in Shakespearean disguise scenes, the dialogue loads the emotional strain on the back of the character in disguise; in *Twelfth Night* and *As You Like It* we watch the flickering expressions on the girls' faces as they keep their lovers under the illusion. Watching a masked character under pressure like this, we sometimes get the impression that the papier-mâché features are moving. Their rigidity increases the pressure on the audience, which is sympathizing with Shen Teh, knowing how hard she must be fighting the impulse to rip the mask off. In reality the actress needs to keep her head fairly still: the mask must move relatively little, but the audience is projecting its own emotions on the immobile features. It is not easy for the reader to visualize the effect.

Even when Yang Sun goes, Shen Teh is not alone, so she has to sustain her impersonation, but she cannot behave consistently.

SHUI TA (*crying out*): The business has gone! He's not in love. This means ruin. I am lost! (*He begins to rush round like a captive animal, continually repeating* "The business has gone!" *until he suddenly stops and addresses* MRS. SHIN.) Mrs. Shin, you grew up in the gutter and so did I. Are we irresponsible? No. Do we lack the necessary brutality?

When she reappears in her own person, Shen Teh again allows herself to be seduced by Yang Sun, in spite of what she knows about him, in spite of knowing she will get herself into trouble again. The understanding she acquires as Shui Ta is of no use to her when she reverts to being a woman.

In fact the whole conception of Shen Teh depends on the amoebalike dichotomy that gives birth to Shui Ta. Her goodness consists of freedom from the vices that are necessary to survive in a world corrupted by the profit motive. But she is no less unrealistically simplified than her anti-type, and her theatrical identity when she isn't wearing a mask is created no more realistically than when she is. On the page, her dialogue can seem facile unless the reader is visualizing the contrast between her two personae and imagining what the actress might sound like and look like, mimicking male toughness both vocally and in her movements.

6

Identity and character

The mistake of psychoanalyzing—The relationship between the parts—Falstaff—Cause and effect

The mistake of psychoanalyzing

It is always a mistake to "psychoanalyze" characters in plays as if they were real people, and it is a mistake we are likelier to make when we are reading than when we are in the theater, reacting to physical impacts, liking her face and his voice, amused by one actor's timing, repelled by another's way of twisting his mouth sideways.

The relationship between the parts

All works of art make their main statement through the relationship between their component parts, but in a painting all the parts are present to the eye at the same moment. In a novel or a play we have to start at the beginning and work our way to the end, which means there are two basic kinds of relationships. We might call these latitudinal and longitudinal. The *latitudinal* relationships are those that exist simultaneously at any one moment of action, while the relationships involving the passage of time are *longitudinal*. It is, for instance, a longitudinal line that connects the Macbeth we meet at the beginning of the play, the brave and successful warrior, with the desperate villain of the last act.

Questions like "How many children had Lady Macbeth?" never bother us in the theater. She says:

> I have given suck, and know
> How tender 'tis to love the babe that milks me—
> I would, while it was smiling in my face,
> Have plucked my nipple from his boneless gums,

And dashed the brains out, had I so sworn as you
Have done to this.

This tells us quite a lot about the latitudinal differences between her and Macbeth; it does not tell us whether she was different when she first became a mother or how long ago it was. And the questions of how many children she had and whether they are still alive do not matter any more than the question, say, of whether Macbeth was good at games when he was a boy. They are irrelevant to both longitudinal and latitudinal relationships between the component parts of the play.

It would be equally senseless to analyze the "character" of Brecht's Shen Teh. The play is a "moral fable," and she is a personification of goodness. She has plenty of theatrical vitality, and we sympathize so much with her in her dilemma that we forget how generalized she is. As a personality she scarcely exists and it is impossible to imagine her as a character in a novel. It would be pointless to speculate about her past or about such questions as whether she derives gratification from dressing up in male clothes. Her character can't be analyzed in terms of repressed aggressions that find no outlet in her normal sex life. We aren't even required to take her seriously as a prostitute. It was an amusing idea of Brecht's to suggest that no one more virtuous could be found, and to let the gods be embarrassed at the danger of compromising themselves by giving her money after accepting her hospitality for the night; but there's no realistic interest in her sexual and financial dealings with her clients.

Is it because Brecht was writing what he called a moral fable that the focus is on human behavior rather than individual character? Or is the playwright *always* more concerned with behavior than with character? Anyway, what does the word "character" mean? It is a dangerous word because it implies a coherence, a consistency, and an individuality, which may not be there. When we read a play, the only evidence we have about a character is the stage directions and the dialogue—what he says and does and what other people say about him and do to him during two hours (or so) of stage action. This is quite enough evidence for constructing an idea of what the play would be like in performance, but not nearly enough evidence—and not the right sort—for constructing an idea of an individual human being whose behavior can be explained in terms of motivations and psychological patterns.

Falstaff

Sir John Falstaff in Shakespeare's *Henry IV Part 1* and *2* is one
of the liveliest, funniest, most richly satisfying characters that a
playwright has ever created. But his vitality has nothing to do
with his being "lifelike," and the impression of richness has
nothing to do with the amount of information that Shakespeare
feeds us about him. He is a composite of theatrical conventions
that derive partly from the medieval English morality plays, in
which riotous behavior would be represented semisymbolically
by a character called Riot. (Today we would hesitate about ap-
plying the word "character" to Riot, or to Gluttony, Lechery,
and the other Deadly Sins who are incarnated in such medieval
plays as *Everyman.*) Falstaff also stems partly from the tradi-
tion of boastful cowards that goes back to classical comedy, and
he is like a clown whose moralizing turns traditional values
upside down. The improvised charade with Hal in *Part 1,* when
Falstaff poses as the King, prepares us for the reassertion of the
moral norm at the end of *Part 2*—the beginning of a new season.

With the circus clown, as with the character stereotypes in
commedia dell'arte (foolish master, crafty servant, etc.), identity
is suggested *visually.* Falstaff is first of all an old man with a
stomach and a complexion that signal disorderly self-indulgence.
Shakespeare is writing ironically when he lets someone so sin-
ful cast so many stones at Bardolph's red nose. Falstaff says:

> I make as good a use of it as many a man doth of a death's
> head or a *memento mori.* I never see thy face but I think of
> hellfire, and Dives that lived in purple, for there he is in his
> robes, burning, burning. If thou wert any way given to vir-
> tue, I would swear by thy face; my oath should be, "by this
> fire, that's God's angel" . . .

Much of Falstaff's vitality derives from the jokes that Shakespeare puts into his mouth; some from the practical jokes that
Prince Hal and his friends play on him. In the highway robbery
sequence, in *Part 1,* Hal and Poins have no difficulty in exposing him as a coward when they put on masks to rob him of the
money he has just stolen from the travelers. But Falstaff is never
at a loss for an excuse:

> By the Lord, I knew ye as well as he that made ye. Why, hear
> you, my masters, was it for me to kill the heir-apparent?

Should I turn upon the true prince? Why, thou knowest I am as valiant as Hercules, but beware instinct—the lion will not touch the true prince. Instinct is a great matter. I was now a coward upon instinct.

None of his excuses, his jokes, or his attempts at moralizing have the effect of individualizing him, but in spite of knowing so little *about* him, we are given the illusion of knowing him extremely well; he quickly becomes an old friend. (As Hamlet and Cordelia do. When they die, we should feel something almost like bereavement.) What Falstaff says, what he does, and what other people say about him substantiate our first impression, fleshing out the cartoon. He is a Humpty Dumpty that all the King's men cannot pull apart, a balloon that cannot be deflated until we are nearly at the end of *Part 2*, when his hopes of becoming the royal favorite are punctured. If Shakespeare had been concerned with the development of an individual character, this final climax, when Falstaff is unable to bounce back as he always has before, would be more important for him than any other. In fact the focus isn't even on him but on the Prince, who has symbolically put aside Folly now that the death of his father has made him rise to the responsibilities of maturity:

I know thee not, old man. Fall to thy prayers.
How ill white hairs become a fool and jester!
I have long dreamed of such a kind of man,
So surfeit-swelled, so old, and so profane;
But, being awaked, I do despise my dream.
Make less thy body hence, and more thy grace,
Leave gormandizing, know the grave doth gape
For thee thrice wider than for other men.
Reply not to me with a fool-born jest,
Presume not that I am the thing I was,
For God doth know, so shall the world perceive,
That I have turned away my former self;
So will I those that kept me company.
When thou dost hear I am as I have been,
Approach me, and thou shalt be as thou wast,
The tutor and the feeder of my riots:
Till then, I banish thee, on pain of death . . .

Can we say that Falstaff is merely a symbolic representation of the riotous inclinations that Hal allows himself as a prince, only to discipline them when he becomes King? No, Falstaff has certainly existed in his own right as a dominant character in earlier scenes, and though he is subsidiary during this long speech, the reader should not forget that part of the audience's attention is focused on his reaction to it. He may even have opened his mouth to speak just before the King says "Reply not . . ." Nor is Falstaff pushed out of the play as summarily as he is dismissed from the King's consciousness. After the royal procession has made its exit, there is a short prose scene with Falstaff, Justice Shallow, Pistol, and Bardolph. Even now the deflation is not total:

> Go with me to dinner: come Lieutenant Pistol, come Bardolph
> —I shall be sent for soon at night.

Immediately after this he is arrested, in verse, by the Lord Chief Justice, and Shakespeare's use of verse to end the play confirms the rejection of Falstaff, whose scenes have all been in prose. He belongs irrevocably to a lower mode of consciousness, while Hal has always been capable of moving upward out of it. This is why he is capable of deciding never again to move downward into it.

So it would be stupid to adopt a "psychoanalytical" approach to Falstaff's "character." We do not need, for instance, to ask ourselves whether childhood deprivations got him into a routine of compulsive overeating. His childhood is as irrelevant as Lady Macbeth's children. His plump presence is essential to the story, but any ideas we may form about his offstage development have nothing to do with the play. To say that Shakespeare's characterization of him is "brilliant" is to say that his identity emerges brilliantly in the context of these two plays. He may appear to exist in sturdy three-dimensionality, but even Shakespeare couldn't resurrect him in a play without Hal. The Falstaff in *The Merry Wives of Windsor* is somebody else of the same shape.

Cause and effect

We could say that Hal develops longitudinally while Falstaff does not. He is no more capable of changing his nature than Riot or Gluttony is. Nor is this merely an example of the survival of medieval stage conventions into Elizabethan drama. Modern plays are equally full of "types"—the oppressive capitalist, the righteous rebel, the generous whore—characters whose behavior is effectively determined by the *type* to which they belong.

Longitudinal and latitudinal relationships necessarily inter-weave very differently in drama from the way they do in a novel. The novel is committed by its form to looking for causal connections between actions. We must feel that we are in a better position to understand the behavior of the characters in Chapter XI if we remember what happened to them in Chapter I. By the end of *War and Peace* Natasha has grown into a plump woman very unlike the girl we met at the beginning, but our sense of knowing her depends on the information we have been fed about her past. In Tolstoy's early fiction he usually provided a full physical description of all the characters on their first appearance, and they remained more or less the same. But the important characters in his mature novels are depicted mainly through other people's reactions to them; and while we progressively come to know them more intimately, another progression is at work as they develop.

The playwright's form pressures him toward selecting fewer incidents and against treating character development causally. When the action of a play is contained within the classical limit of twenty-four hours, it is impossible for the characters to develop very much. Even in an epic play that spans twenty years, character development will probably conform to a fairly simple scheme.

With any work of art it may be difficult to distinguish between the pattern the artist has constructed deliberately and the pattern we see when we look at it. Our instinct is always to interpret, to arrive at an understanding of a new perception by fitting it into the framework of concepts we have used for ordering our previous experience. "What is it?" we say, when a child shows us a drawing. However unrealistic a play is, we always tend to look for patterns, causal relationships, motivations, which we can interpret by referring to our knowledge of human behavior. We are also liable to make moral judgments. Cordelia is no more of a "character" than Falstaff, but we are prone to ask ourselves such questions as "Couldn't she have been a bit more considerate of the old man's feelings when he was asking for reassurance about how much she loved him?"

When we read a play the experience tends to be more intellectual and less emotional than it is in the theater, and we are more disposed to *interpret,* more eagerly on the lookout for explicable relationships between the component parts of the text. With Cordelia, we would do well to remember that much of the explanation we are looking for is to be found in the actress's (or boy actor's) appearance of innocence—a white dress may play an important part in determining our reaction to her. With Falstaff or with Shui Ta it may be determined largely by the actor's padded paunch or the actress's severe-looking male mask.

Even when the playwright wants to weave universal forces into his text—Nature, the gods, destiny—he will do it through the characters' experience and the other evidence that can be put in front of us physically. When the action is confined to personal relationships, the actor's face and personality may function almost like a mask, at least in the sense of precluding any question of how the character became what he is. The plot may demonstrate (as in *Oedipus*) that the gods destined the hero to do what he has done and to become what he is, or (as in Ibsen's *Ghosts*) it may show that the hero has inherited his physical and mental traits from his father or mother; but it is still the actor's face, makeup, and physique that persuade us to take it for granted that the character is the sort of man he looks like. It may then turn out to be the play's function to disabuse us—to unmask him. The Nurse in *The Father* is not what she seems. Shakespeare's interest in Prince Hal's development may seem to be spread over a longish period, but there is little realistic detail in it and the moment of conversion, which comes when he rejects Falstaff, is almost as abrupt as the dropping of a mask or the revelation of a ducal costume under a drab disguise.

Looking at printed words in a playscript, we're likely to assimilate the characterization more in terms of static type than of developing individuality. Unlike the novelist, the playwright is envisaging a performance, so he is not trying to put words together in a way that will directly convey an illusion of human personality. But we may respond by piecing the stage directions and the lines of dialogue together to construct a tentative portrait, which we can adapt as we collect more evidence. From the beginning we are probably asking ourselves questions like "Is Jerry the sort of man who . . ." "Is Lady Macbeth the sort of woman who . . ." Outside the theater we may be far more resistant to the notion of human typology, but inside we would find ourselves accepting the convention that links identity to type, behavior to appearance. Today it would be as hard as ever to satisfy an audience with a play in which the sympathetic characters were ugly and the villains attractive.

7

Irony and ambiguity

Irony in the forum—In the nineteenth-century parlor

Irony in the forum

In the sequences we took from *The Cherry Orchard* and *The Father*, there was a wide gap between words and underlying intentions, though the characters were not being consciously ironical. But when Shakespeare's Mark Antony insists that "Brutus is an honorable man," he does not want to be believed. Even a reader unfamiliar with *Julius Caesar* would soon realize how the actor could let out the throttle on his scorn through the rhetorical repetitions of the phrase. Brutus, who had the chance to address the crowd first, spoke declamatorily but in prose:

> Romans, countrymen, and lovers! hear me for my cause, and be silent, that you may hear: believe me for mine honor, and have respect to mine honor, that you may believe.

Antony's speech is in verse, which helps the actor to point the deliberateness of the phrasing, while the rhythm makes the repetitions more striking than they could be in prose. The irony in the first reference to "the noble Brutus" would not be apparent to the unsuspecting reader, but Antony has no sooner used the word "honorable," than he puts it, effectively, into inverted commas by repeating it in the next line:

> (For Brutus is an honorable man;
> So are they all; all honorable men)

If we are prompted to glance back at the beginning of Brutus's speech, we see that he repeated the word "honor" as soon as he used it, implicitly suggesting that honor is the crucial issue. After three more "honorables" and six more mentions of Brutus's name, Antony can easily put his initial praise of the *noble* Brutus into an ironic perspective with a scathing pun about "brutish beasts." The first part of Antony's speech ends when he breaks off to weep. He resumes after brief speeches from four of the Plebeians have enabled him to gauge their reactions. The two new allusions to "honorable men" are blatantly ironic, so the reader, by turning backward and forward over about two pages, could see how the hidden intention is determining the actor's tone.

In the nineteenth-century parlor

Some passages of dialogue are much harder to construe without the mediating actor, especially when the playwright is making his characters talk guardedly, with deliberate ambiguity. In Ibsen's *Hedda Gabler*, for instance, during the second conversation between Hedda and Judge Brack, it is obvious that they both mean more than they are saying, but how much more? Even after reading to the end of the play and turning back to reread the more difficult passages, it is hard to be sure.

At the end of the first act, Tesman, the spectacled, plump, 33-year-old husband, has been pleading with his new wife, the 29-year-old Hedda, not to play with the pistols that belonged to her father, General Gabler. As the lights go up on the second act, she is loading one of them and shouting out of the French windows to the 45-year-old judge, who is—perhaps symbolically—using the back way into the house. Teasingly threatening to shoot him, she aims at him and fires, deliberately missing, but deliberately alarming him. This prepares, theatrically, for the verbal dueling that is to follow. Brack says it was stupid of him not to have realized Hedda would be alone in the house. He should have come earlier. Instead of withdrawing, as we might have expected, into cold politeness, she confides in him about the excruciating boredom she endured on her honeymoon while Tesman was researching in libraries and copying out old parchments. She is obviously not in love with him or she wouldn't say:

And there's nothing exactly ridiculous about him. Is there?

For someone so proud, she is surprisingly eager to explain why she accepted his offer of marriage:

BRACK (*looks at her a little uncertainly*): I thought you believed, like everyone else, that he would become a very prominent man.

HEDDA (*looks tired*): Yes, I did. And when he came and begged me on his bended knees to be allowed to love and to cherish me, I didn't see why I shouldn't let him.

BRACK: No, well—if one looks at it like that—

HEDDA: It was more than my other admirers were prepared to do, Judge dear.

BRACK (*laughs*): Well, I can't answer for the others. As far as I myself am concerned, you know I've always had a considerable respect for the institution of marriage. As an institution.

HEDDA (*lightly*): Oh, I've never entertained any hopes of you.

BRACK: All I want is to have a circle of friends whom I can trust, whom I can help with advice or—or by any other means, and into whose houses I may come and go as a—trusted friend.

HEDDA: Of the husband?

BRACK (*bows*): Preferably, to be frank, of the wife. And of the husband too, of course. Yes, you know, this kind of triangle is a delightful arrangement for all parties concerned.

HEDDA: Yes, I often longed for a third person while I was away. Oh, those hours we spent alone in railway compartments—

BRACK: Fortunately your honeymoon is now over.

HEDDA (*shakes her head*): There's a long, long way still to go. I've only reached a stop on the line.

BRACK: Why not jump out and stretch your legs a little, Mrs. Hedda?

HEDDA: I'm not the jumping sort.

BRACK: Aren't you?

HEDDA: No. There's always someone around who—

BRACK (*laughs*): Who looks at one's legs?

HEDDA: Yes. Exactly.

BRACK: Well, but surely—

HEDDA (*with a gesture of rejection*): I don't like it. I'd rather stay where I am. Sitting in the compartment. *A deux.*

BRACK: But suppose a third person were to step into the compartment?

HEDDA: That would be different.

BRACK: A trusted friend—someone who understood—

HEDDA: And was lively and amusing—

BRACK: And interested in—more subjects than one—

HEDDA (*sighs audibly*): Yes, that'd be a relief.

BRACK (*hears the front door open and shut*): The triangle is com-
   pleted.
HEDDA (*half under her breath*): And the train goes on.

Stage directions like *"laughing," "lightly,"* or *"sighs audibly"* do
not help us to understand the hidden language. Does Hedda
want Brack to think she might have been interested in an offer
of marriage from him? Does he want her to think that he is not
interested in her sexually? Is he really not interested in her sexually, or is he interested in friendship mainly as a stepping-stone?
What kind of triangular relationship does she have in mind? Is
each of them understanding what the other intends and intend-
ing what the other understands? Are they calculating seriously
how much they want to reveal of their feelings and intentions,
or being diverted into an appealingly dangerous game of flirta-
tion? How much are they each staking and how much more
would they be prepared to stake?

The dialogue is highly ambiguous, whether you read the play
or watch it in performance, but the two sets of ambiguities are
quite different. The reader's only evidence is Ibsen's words, but
the audience is watching a man and a woman together. Each
pause, each hesitation, each inflection, each movement of the
head, the hand, the body is providing evidence, which is blended
with the words before they reach us. We have no time to extri-
cate our interpretation of what is happening from the director's
and actors' interpretation of the text. The meaning of a phrase
can depend on tone, timing, phrasing, on how she is looking at
him, how close he is to her, whether her hand touches his. The
actors are interpreting the script in two ways—involuntarily and
voluntarily. The involuntary element arises directly out of their
personalities—some are naturally more outgoing and seductive
than others. What they can control, within the limits of their technique, is the use they make of their voices, eyes, face muscles,
physique. For each syllable, dozens of tones and movements are
available to them, and the choices they make will be based mainly
on the work done with the director and the rest of the cast during
the rehearsal period. So the audience is looking at the end-product
of a long period of interpretative work, whereas the reader new
to the play knows nothing about Brack except what he has learned
from the previous act. According to Ibsen's stage direction,

JUDGE BRACK *is forty-five; rather short, but well built and elas-
   tic in his movements. He has a roundish face with an aristocratic*

profile. His hair, cut short, is still almost black, and is carefully barbered. Eyes lively and humorous. Thick eyebrows. His mustache is also thick, and is trimmed square at the ends. He is wearing outdoor clothes which are elegant but a little too youthful for him. He has a monocle in one eye; now and then he lets it drop.

Tesman's conversation with his aunt has also revealed that the Judge helped to make arrangements for them to buy the house on easy terms. This action could have been motivated by his interest in Hedda.

The reader's interpretation of the sequence is based on his knowledge of the preceding text; the actors' interpretation is based on the whole play. They know that Hedda is going to kill herself when Brack is in a strategically advantageous position. He finds out that she has given one of her pistols to Eilert Loevborg, who shot himself with it. It is now in the possession of the police, who are trying to trace the owner. Unless Brack keeps silent, Hedda will have to appear in court together with the madam of the brothel where Eilert killed himself. Brack promises not to abuse the power he now has over her, but Tesman will be out every evening, working on the manuscript of Eilert's book with Mrs. Elvsted, so Brack will be "the only cock on the dunghill," as Hedda puts it in her last words before she shoots herself. He hadn't expected her to take this way out of her dilemma and he hadn't deliberately set about creating it for her. It is even possible that he intended to keep his promise about not abusing his power. Ibsen's intention was that each passage of dialogue should be filtered through the actors' personalities and performances. The ambiguities remain, but they are not nearly so wide open as they are for the reader.

Is this openness a disadvantage? Undeniably it makes for difficulties during the first reading, when it is hard to cope with the variety of options the text offers, but for the reader who is willing to take time and trouble, the experience can be fascinating. He even has an advantage over the director in the theater in that he does not have to find a single practical solution to every problem. The action going on inside his imagination is more like a rehearsal than a performance, in that he can stop it whenever he wants to make his actors experiment with an alternative inflection or emphasis. He may even recast a role in the middle of a sentence, deciding, for instance, to make Hedda taller, slimmer, more deliberate in her speech, and less attractive.

8

Mental theater

Where to put the stress—Mental scene-changes

The advantages and disadvantages of mental theater are analo-
gous to the advantages and disadvantages of mental arithmetic:
there is a limit to the complexity of the calculations you can make
in your head, but there is no limit to the amount of alterations
you can make without creating a mess.

Where to put the stress

The example from *Hedda Gabler* showed us that a text may be
offering a wide variety of options. Taking a simpler example,
let's, for a moment, ignore all the visual factors, considering only
the use of voice. In the thirteen-word question

> Surely you aren't telling me to go because they might arrive
> together again?

there is only one word that could not be loaded with the main
stress—the word "to." The twelve possible stresses are equally
legitimate and they produce twelve meanings, which aren't entirely different but aren't exactly the same. If you heard the line
performed in a play, it wouldn't occur to you that in settling on
one reading the actor had rejected eleven others, and even if it
did, you wouldn't have time to work out what the others were.
There is also the question of how heavy the stress is, and of
whether one of the other words is to be spoken with a stress that,
though subordinate, gives the word more weight than the other
eleven. And we still haven't touched on the various possibilities
of tone, tempo, and rhythm. The speaker could be sympathetic
or sarcastic, concerned or indifferent, amused or exasperated.

If you can be as dependent as this on the director and the actor
with thirteen words, how much greater is the part they play in
interpreting a whole script?

There is plenty of scope for obscurity and ambiguity in the novel. Critics often disagree violently in their interpretations, but it is much easier for the writer to be explicit about what is going on inside the characters' minds. He can tell us when one understands, misinterprets, or fails to grasp what the other is saying or not saying, and he can explain the deductions each makes from the other's behavior. The playwright may choose to write *"lying," "smiling,"* or *"hesitating"* as a stage direction, but there is a narrow limit to the amount of information he can convey like this. The medium tends to push him toward making his statements through the dialogue and leaving it to be interpreted differently in each production. This could be called a limitation of the medium, but a great artist can usually turn limitations into advantages. The richness of Shakespeare's, Chekhov's, and the best of Ibsen's texts lies partly in ambiguities, which only the careful reader can fully explore.

Mental scene-changes

Though it is generally an advantage to envisage a performance on a stage, the imagination is flexible enough to adapt a sequence of the play into a film when the playwright has been limited by his medium in a negative way. Reading Ibsen's *Rosmersholm*, why shouldn't you picture John Rosmer and Rebecca West as they throw themselves into the mill-race? Why restrict yourself to the housekeeper who is looking out of the window and soliloquizing for the benefit of the audience?

> MRS. HELSETH: The carriage, miss, is——. (*Looks around the room.*) Not here? Out together at this time of night? Well, well—I must say—! Hm! (*Goes out into the hall, looks around and comes in again.*) Not sitting on the bench— ah, well! (*Goes to the window and looks out.*) Good heavens! What is that white thing—! As I am a living soul, they are both out on the footbridge! God forgive the sinful creatures—if they are not in each other's arms! (*Gives a wild scream.*) Ah!—they are over—both of them! Over into the mill-race! Help! Help! (*Her knees tremble, she holds on shakily to the back of a chair and can scarcely get her words out.*) No. No help here. The dead woman has taken them.

This melodramatic speech is a poor substitute for a direct dra-
matization of the double suicide.

Chekhov had more mastery over his medium than Ibsen, and
it is hardly ever a disadvantage in his work that offstage events
and objects remain invisible. It is good that we see no more than
a glimpse of the cherry orchard through the window; it might
be even better if we saw nothing of it. The reality that the scene-
painter can give to it is less important than the reality it acquires
through the dialogue, which shows clearly how each of the characters remembers it in a different way. Madam Ranevsky feels
nostalgic about the pleasure in the blossom-scented sunlight;
Lopakhin is aware that a valuable part of the estate has never
been commercially exploited. A film of *The Cherry Orchard,*
which ended with woodcutters hacking at the beautiful trees,
would be showing us something that is better left unseen.

What about the descriptions of offstage action in Shakespearean
monologues? When you read the final sequence in Act Four,
Scene Seven of *Hamlet,* do you visualize the Queen as she talks
and Laertes and the King as they react? Or do you see the picture that her words evoke?

> There is a willow grows aslant the brook,
> That shows his hoar leaves in the glassy stream,
> There with fantastic garlands did she come
> Of crow-flowers, nettles, daisies, and long purples
> That liberal shepherds give a grosser name,
> But our cold maids do dead men's fingers call them.
> There on the pendent boughs her crownet weeds
> Clamb'ring to hang, an envious sliver broke,
> When down her weedy trophies and herself
> Fell in the weeping brook. Her clothes spread wide,
> And mermaid-like awhile they bore her up,
> Which time she chanted snatches of old lauds,
> As one incapable of her own distress,
> Or like a creature native and indued
> Unto that element. But long it could not be
> Till that her garments, heavy with their drink,
> Pulled the poor wretch from her melodious lay
> To muddy death.

The description is so graphic that even in the theater, with
three well-lit actors in front of us, the stage picture is partly dis-
placed by the picture that the words paint. Without ceasing to

see the Queen, we also see the drowning Ophelia. Without ceasing to listen to the words, we also hear the dying girl's song. When we are reading, the balance between the two pictures and the two sets of sounds may be different, but all four should be present to our imagination. Watching Laurence Olivier's film of *Hamlet,* we may have thought it was a bad lapse of taste to show a horizontal Jean Simmons floating decorously among the tangled leaves and waterweeds, but the imaginary film sequences we interpolate into our armchair reading will accord perfectly with our own taste.

9

Silence

Looking for silence—How to manage without signposts—Silence alongside speech—Silence and the contemporary playwright— Pressures toward silence—The silent killer

As Susan Sontag has pointed out, "Much of the beauty of Harpo Marx's muteness derives from his being surrounded by manic talkers." One of the disadvantages of reading a play is that, not being surrounded by manic talkers, we find it tremendously hard to remember how powerful the theatrical effect of silence can be. Unlike silence in the room where we're reading, silence in a performance can exist only as an interruption to the sound. If action is going on, it will derive a special quality from the silence. The sequence may be building toward a climax, and the silence may play an important part in the progression. Even two seconds of hesitation before the word "yes" makes it stronger than it would otherwise be, and the effect of the brief silence is inseparable from that of the yes. A prolonged silence can work powerfully if it starts out of a tension and doesn't last long enough to destroy it.

The three basic problems for the reader are
1. to know where the silences come,
2. to gauge their length,
3. to imagine their effect.

Looking for silence

It is easy enough to spot the silences when the writer gives us some such stage direction as *"After a pause"* or *"Hesitating."* No playwright can ever have been more scrupulous than Harold Pinter in specifying his requirements. Here is a sequence from the first act of *The Caretaker*. Aston, who lives in a house as full as a lumber room with useless objects, has come home with a

shabbily dressed old man, Davies, who indicates that he often
sleeps in the open air.

DAVIES: Nothing but wind then.
  (*Pause.*)
ASTON: Yes, when the wind gets up it. . . .
  (*Pause.*)
DAVIES: Yes. . . .
ASTON: Mmmmn. . . .
  (*Pause.*)
DAVIES: Gets very draughty.
ASTON: Ah.
DAVIES: I'm very sensitive to it.
ASTON: Are you?
DAVIES: Always have been.
  (*Pause.*)
  You got more rooms then, have you?
ASTON: Where?
DAVIES: I mean, along the landing here . . . up the landing
  there.
ASTON: They're out of commission.
DAVIES: Get away.
ASTON: They need a lot of doing to.
  (*Slight pause.*)
DAVIES: What about downstairs?
ASTON: That's closed up. Needs seeing to. . . . The floors. . . .
  (*Pause.*)
DAVIES: I was lucky you come into that caff. I might have been
  done by that Scotch git. I been left for dead more than
  once.
  (*Pause.*)
  I noticed that there was someone was living in the house
  next door.
ASTON: What?
DAVIES (*gesturing*): I noticed. . . .
ASTON: Yes. There's people living all along the road.
DAVIES: Yes, I noticed the curtains pulled down there next
  door as we come along.
ASTON: They're neighbours.
  (*Pause.*)
DAVIES: This your house then, is it?
  (*Pause.*)

ASTON: I'm in charge.
DAVIES: You the landlord, are you?
   (*He puts a pipe in his mouth and puffs without lighting it.*)
   Yes, I noticed them heavy curtains pulled across next door
   as we come along.

The careless reader may take little notice of these stage directions, thinking: "Oh, that's something for the actor." It's also
something for the reader, who needs as much information as he
can get, not only from the words but from the spaces between
them. In this passage Pinter has used five different indications
for the duration of the pause. Four dots suggests a longer pause
than three dots; "*Pause*" a longer one than "*Slight pause.*" There
is also the final stage direction, which suggests quite a prolonged
pause, coming as it does in the middle of a speech, immediately
after a question, which is left unanswered. The reader cannot yet
know that uncertainty about who is the landlord will be a major
cause of anxiety to Davies, but Pinter obviously wants it to be
noticeable that Aston is not answering the old man's question.
   The shorter pauses are important for different reasons. They
stress the discontinuity of the conversation, which indicates that
in their different ways the two men are both embarrassed with
each other, and that their preoccupations do not seem to inter-
lock. The visual puzzle set by their appearance together is not
being explained by the emergence of a plot in which Aston plans
to make use of Davies. On the contrary, the halting, inconse-
quential conversation suggests that the play is not going to generate much suspense of the usual kind. This in itself increases
our mystification about how we are going to be kept entertained
for the next two hours.
   At the same time, the pauses are helping to characterize the
two men, emphasizing not only their shyness but their inarticu-
lateness and the difficulties each has in following any line of
thought, even if he has begun it himself. Aston does not know
how to finish the sentence that starts "When the wind gets up
it . . ." and he cannot explain what is wrong with the floors downstairs. Davies does not want to go on talking about the times he
has been left for dead and the pause before his next sentence
heightens the absurdity of it. That someone is living in the house
next door would not be worth mentioning unless he were desperate for something to say, and when Aston says "What?" he is
reduced to a gesture and another unfinished sentence.

How to manage without signposts

Most playwrights are less scrupulous than Pinter in signaling where the silences come and how long they last. Some of the best playwrights, like Shakespeare, give very little information in stage directions. Their dialogue invariably contains all the help we need, but we have to work a little harder to make sure we don't miss it. We must always be on the lookout for questions that (like "You the landlord, are you?") remain unanswered. Another indication of a pause is a request that is ignored. In Act One, Scene Two of *Hamlet*, the King opposes the Prince's declared intention of going back to Wittenberg:

> It is most retrograde to our desire,
> And we beseech you, bend you to remain
> Here in the cheer and comfort of our eye,
> Our chiefest courtier, cousin, and our son.
> QUEEN: Let not your mother lose her prayers, Hamlet, I pray
> thee stay with us, go not to Wittenberg.
> HAMLET: I shall in all my best obey you, madam.
> KING: Why 'tis a loving and a fair reply . . .

In a hasty reading it might not be apparent that there is a pause after "our son." The whole court would be waiting with curiosity for Hamlet's reply to the King. The Queen speaks to prevent the silence from becoming too awkward, but the audience must register the awkwardness first. In replying to her, Hamlet still ignores the King, who then decides to ignore the snub. To clarify this it may be necessary to introduce another, briefer, pause after "madam." It may cost the King some slight effort to respond so blandly to such rudeness. Or it may not. This is one of the options that Shakespeare leaves open to the actor.

The reader should also be on the alert for speeches that begin in the middle of a blank verse line. In his mature plays Shakespeare never breaks the line without a good reason, and sometimes the reason is the need for a pause. In the final scene of *Measure for Measure*, soon after the Duke has thrown off his disguise, he condemns Angelo to death for abusing his authority. He has threatened Isabella that unless she sleeps with him, her brother, Claudio, will be executed for inchastity. When Mariana, Angelo's wife, pleads for her husband's life, Isabella does not yet know that Claudio is still alive:

MARIANA: O, Isabel . . . will you not lend a knee?
DUKE: He dies for Claudio's death.
ISABELLA: Most bounteous sir,
　Look, if it pleases you, on this man condemned
　As if my brother lived.

Peter Brook achieved tremendous suspense in his 1951 production of the play at Stratford-on-Avon by making Isabella hesitate in an agony of indecision before kneeling down to plead for
the man who has wronged her.

Another sign of the need for a pause is a change of tone. In
an earlier scene (Act Three, Scene One) in *Measure for Measure,* Isabella tells Claudio about Angelo's threat. She does not
intend to submit:

ISABELLA: Be ready, Claudio, for your death tomorrow.
CLAUDIO: Yes. Has he affections in him,
　That thus can make him bite the law by th' nose,
　When he would force it? Sure it is no sin—
　Or of the deadly seven it is the least.

There are two changes of subject (and of tone) in Claudio's short
speech. The "Yes" is an apparently resigned response to Isabella's
admonition. The question shifts to speculation about the human
emotions of the man who can manipulate the law in his sexual
blackmail. The last sentence is a general speculation about for-
nication: Claudio is thinking both of the offense he has committed in sleeping with Juliet and of the way Angelo would be
jeopardizing his own salvation if Isabella submitted to him. The
three sections of the speech should be separated by pauses.

The fact that Claudio's first blank verse line is incomplete
suggests that there should also be a pause before the "Yes." It is
not easy to say yes to a command like this one.

Silence alongside speech

There is another kind of silence that is easily forgotten—the
silence that exists (like Harpo Marx's) alongside speech. There
is nearly always more than one character onstage, and if they all
talked at the same time we'd understand nothing. One way of
judging an actor's quality is to watch how he listens. A very small
movement or a change of rhythm or the inhibition of a move-

ment already in progress can be more telling than a demonstrative reaction.

A good playwright, like Chekhov, works continually through the complex of pressures that the actors will exert on each other, not just through words but underneath and around them. A movement across the stage or a refusal to look someone else in the eye or to respond to a provocation can say as much as a line of dialogue.

The main climax in Act Three of *The Cherry Orchard* is the revelation that Lopakhin has bought the estate, but it is difficult for the reader to gauge the theatrical impact of the news because Chekhov, as so often, is making more capital out of what his characters do not say than of what they do. Without lapsing into silence, they tread delicately around the edge of it, talking about irrelevant trivialities or complaining that they feel tired.

It is characteristic of Madam Ranevsky that she should be holding a party on the evening her estate is up for sale, and the two-edged mood is established for the whole of the third act as the curtain goes up on the orchestra, which is playing in the vestibule while couples come dancing downstage into the drawing room. Varya, partnered by the Station Master, is weeping quietly, wiping away her tears as she dances. Gayev, Madam Ranevsky's brother, should have arrived back from town: unless the auction has not taken place, the estate must have been sold by now, but it is just possible that he has bought it himself with the power of attorney and the money their great-aunt sent from Yaroslavl. Later on, Anya, Madam Ranevsky's daughter, comes in with news from the kitchen. An old man said the orchard had been sold, but went away without saying who bought it.

Like Shakespeare, Chekhov often works comedy into the most dramatic moments, and Lopakhin is greeted on his entrance with an accidental blow from the stick Varya has been brandishing at Yepikhodov, the accident-prone clerk. Lopakhin and Gayev have traveled back together from the auction, but Gayev has not yet appeared, and instead of coming out with the news that everyone is waiting for, Lopakhin grumbles about the bump on his head, about a feeling of dizziness, which may be due partly to brandy, and about missing the train on the return journey. As in the scene with the Porter in *Macbeth*, the comedy of procrastination is preparing for a climax that may be tragic. When Gayev enters, wiping away tears, he seems equally disinclined to talk about the auction, though Ranevsky, who is also in tears, implores him to tell her quickly. He makes a gesture of resignation and, still weeping, hands over parcels of shopping. The anchovies and the Black Sea herrings remind him how hungry he is. Still without answering the question, he goes off to his own quarters, ordering Firs, the old manservant, to help him change his clothes. It is only after all this that the climax is detonated, when Ranevsky puts two direct questions to Lopakhin:

MRS. RANEVSKY: Was the cherry orchard sold?
LOPAKHIN: It was.
MRS. RANEVSKY: Who bought it?
LOPAKHIN: I did.

All the previous talk has been necessary to the characters as a smokescreen and to the writer as a buildup, elaborate but not overextended.

Gayev and Lopakhin had different reasons for not wanting to talk about the auction. Gayev was grief-stricken and guilty about his ineffectuality in preventing the loss of the family's estate, while Lopakhin, according to the stage direction, was *"embarrassed, fearing to betray his delight."* His silence was also the culmination of the confusion he registered in the play's opening moments. After staying up to meet the family at the station, he fell asleep in an armchair. He has been well disposed toward Madam Ranevsky ever since he was a boy of fifteen, when she was kind to him after his father had clouted his ear, and throughout the first two acts he has importuned her with well-meant advice about making the orchard into plots for summer bungalows. Now he is the beneficiary of the inertia from which he failed to budge her. An extraordinary theatrical effect is gained out of the two men's reluctance to talk. A playwright less sensitive to ambivalence—and less adept at exteriorizing it—might have given Lopakhin a gloating entrance that would have pricked the bubble too quickly. Victorian melodramas that rush simplistically from one climax to the next are easier to read but much less interesting.

With *The Cherry Orchard* the reader should resist the inclination to concentrate least on the characters who say least and he should keep trying to visualize the changing focus of the stage picture. As soon as Lopakhin comes in, he is the center of attention. Wherever he sits or stands, this must become the dominant position because the other characters, hanging on his words, will gravitate toward him and group themselves around him. By the time Gayev enters, it is clear that Lopakhin doesn't want to talk, so their curiosity now fastens itself onto Gayev, who remains dominant only briefly because he remains onstage only briefly. His exit shifts the center of gravity back to Lopakhin, who is once again the only character onstage in possession of the information they all want. Just as the onstage characters are focusing first on Lopakhin, then on Gayev, then on Lopakhin again, irrespective of who else is speaking, so are the spectators in the auditorium. In *Measure for Measure,* when the Duke was revealed under the Friar's habit, there was one abrupt shift in the focus of the stage picture; here there are three. It is not easy for the reader to make sufficient allowance for this.

Even in a play like *Hedda Gabler,* where Ibsen grants his heroine a preeminence Chekhov does not allow to any of his characters in *The Cherry Orchard,* it is all too easy for the reader to concentrate on what is being said by other characters, forgetting to visualize Hedda's silent reactions. The more subtly a play's ironies are developed, the less necessary it becomes for points to be made explicitly, and when Judge Brack brings the news of Eilert Loevborg's suicide, there is no need for Hedda to say very much. The inept and uncomprehending reactions of the others work almost like spotlights, forcing us to concentrate on her expression:

HEDDA: Eilert Loevborg has settled his account with life. He's had the courage to do what—what he had to do.

MRS. ELVSTED: No, that's not why it happened. He did it because he was mad.

TESMAN: He did it because he was desperate.

HEDDA: You're wrong! I know!

MRS. ELVSTED: He must have been mad. The same as when he tore up the manuscript.

BRACK (*starts*): Manuscript? Did he tear it up?

MRS. ELVSTED: Yes. Last night.

TESMAN (*whispers*): Oh, Hedda, we shall never be able to escape from this.

BRACK: Hm. Strange.

TESMAN (*wanders around the room*): To think of Eilert dying like that. And not leaving behind him the thing that would have made his name endure.

MRS. ELVSTED: If only it could be pieced together again!

TESMAN: Yes, yes, yes! If only it could! I'd give anything—

MRS. ELVSTED: Perhaps it can, Mr. Tesman.

TESMAN: What do you mean?

MRS. ELVSTED (*searches in the pocket of her dress*): Look. I kept the notes he dictated it from.

HEDDA (*takes a step nearer*): Ah!

TESMAN: You kept them, Mrs. Elvsted! What?

MRS. ELVSTED: Yes, here they are. I brought them with me when I left home. They've been in my pocket ever since.

TESMAN: Let me have a look.

MRS. ELVSTED (*hands him a wad of small sheets of paper*): They're in a terrible muddle. All mixed up.

TESMAN: I say, just fancy if we could sort them out! Perhaps if we work on them together—?

MRS. ELVSTED: Oh, yes! Let's try, anyway!

TESMAN: We'll manage it. We must! I shall dedicate my life to this.

HEDDA: You, George? Your life?

TESMAN: Yes—well, all the time I can spare. My book'll have to wait. Hedda, you do understand? What? I owe it to Eilert's memory.

HEDDA: Perhaps.

TESMAN: Well, my dear Mrs. Elvsted, you and I'll have to pool our brains. No use crying over spilt milk, what? We must try to approach this matter calmly.

MRS. ELVSTED: Yes, yes, Mr. Tesman. I'll do my best.

TESMAN: Well, come over here and let's start looking at these notes right away. Where shall we sit? Here? No, the other room. You'll excuse us, won't you, Judge? Come along with me, Mrs. Elvsted.

Tesman knows already that it was Hedda who destroyed the manuscript, but he does not know the reason. She made out that it was for his sake, so that his reputation should not be eclipsed. Neither he nor she is going to disabuse the others, who still think Eilert tore up the book himself. Hedda cannot give any of them a hint of how much Eilert meant to her, though one of the forces pushing her toward suicide is the irony of her husband's sheepish decision to devote his life to the memory of her former rival. He is partly motivated by eagerness to expiate her guilt in destroying a masterpiece out of loving concern for his reputation.

Hedda is condemned to silence, even when she realizes that the innocuous-looking Thea Elvsted, deprived of her man, is being presented with the same stepping-stones in a relationship with Tesman. The progress from amanuensis to inspiration to mistress may be quite an easy one, especially with Hedda out of the way. The better the actress who plays Hedda, the more subtly her changing expressions register the ironies, which are too complex for a reader to take in without turning to the end of the play and then turning back to this passage—not to study the words but the spaces in between them. Hedda's "Ah" is a sign of nervousness on Ibsen's part, as if even the actress might need a reminder that she mustn't stop acting just because she isn't talking. Her silent reaction is more important than the words she's reacting to; nor should we forget Brack's reactions when he is not speaking.

Silence and the contemporary playwright

It could be said that twentieth-century writers have delved further than their predecessors into the theatrical possibilities of silence. Beckett and Pinter are probably the two most important of the playwrights whose technique has been influenced in its development by experience of radio drama, where silence simply negates a character. In Pinter's first radio play, *A Slight Ache*, there is one character whose very existence is uncertain. After hearing a husband and wife talking to each other about a matchseller, we hear each of them talking to him and becoming increasingly irrational as he fails to answer. They offer him more and more of what they own and give away more and more about themselves, but we never find out whether he has any "real" existence outside their imagination. His silence, in any case, is acting as a powerful catalyst on the action.

Pressures toward silence

Pinter's first full-length play, *The Birthday Party*, moves ineluctably toward a climax in which the central character is reduced to a theatrical impotence, which is expressed by a silence quite unlike that of the powerful matchseller. Meg, the landlady in the squalid seaside boardinghouse, chats incessantly, but unlike her husband, Petey, who responds monosyllabically, Stanley begins by talking back to her. It is the two sinister visitors to the boardinghouse, Goldberg and McCann, who reduce him to silence. We see them trying to intimidate him in several sequences during Act Two, but we never learn what happens offstage.

The hardest sequence for the reader to picture is crucial to the third act, which builds up slowly toward Stanley's entrance. We get our first indication that something unusual is happening when Petey discourages Meg from going up to call him. When she went up earlier, she was intercepted by McCann, Goldberg's Irish henchman. Now they are both in the room with him. Next we learn that a big car is waiting outside. Alone with Goldberg, Petey asks how Stanley is. Goldberg talks cheerfully but evasively about his "nervous breakdown." The suggestion that Goldberg and McCann may have induced it is strengthened by McCann's qualms. He tells Goldberg he's not prepared to go back into Stanley's room, and there are sinister overtones in the mention of Goldberg's friend Monty as the doctor best suited to treat Stanley. Goldberg seems anxious to get rid of Petey before Stanley comes downstairs; Petey seems too concerned about Stanley to hurry off to work. A comic diversion is provided by Goldberg's scene with Lulu, the girl he seduced the night before, but most of the act is building steadily toward Stanley's entrance:

> MCCANN *goes to the door, left, and goes out. He ushers in* STANLEY, *who is dressed in striped trousers, black jacket, and white collar. He carries a bowler hat in one hand and his broken glasses in the other. He is clean-shaven.* MCCANN *follows and closes the door.* GOLDBERG *meets* STANLEY, *seats him in a chair, right, and puts his hat on the table.*

A cursory reading of the stage direction may not be enough to form an impression of the impact made by the change in Stanley's appearance. Previously he has always looked slovenly, unshaven and not very clean. We first saw him coming down to breakfast in spectacles and a pajama jacket. But in becoming clean and neat, he seems to have lost the knack of taking any initiative. He is the main focus of audience attention as Goldberg and McCann talk to him, simulating concern, while he remains impassive. Goldberg's initial questions are like pebbles dropped into water that make no plopping sound.

> How are you, Stan?
> *Pause.*

Are you feeling any better?
Pause.
What's the matter with your glasses?
GOLDBERG *bends to look.*
They're broken. A pity.
STANLEY *stares blankly at the floor.*

In the long ensuing sequence he remains silent, not even moving or reacting as they bombard him with banter—no doubt from positions on either side of him, which would normally be theatrically subordinate.

> GOLDBERG: From now on, we'll be the hub of your wheel.
> McCANN: We'll renew your season ticket.
> GOLDBERG: We'll take tuppence off your morning tea.
> McCANN: We'll give you a discount on all inflammable goods.
> GOLDBERG: We'll watch over you.
> McCANN: Advise you.

They go on in this vein for so long that it's quite hard, even in the theater, to be sure of whether they're trying to break Stanley down still further or are merely playing with him, like two cats with a mouse they've crippled. The sequence culminates in direct questions, which forces Stanley into a desperate effort to speak. First his head lifts very slowly to turn toward Goldberg. Then, according to the stage direction,

> STANLEY *begins to clench and unclench his eyes.*

In the subsequent stage directions,

> STANLEY's *hands clutching his glasses begin to tremble . . .*
> STANLEY *concentrates, his mouth opens, he attempts to speak, fails and emits sounds from his throat . . . They watch him. He draws a long breath which shudders down his body. He concentrates . . . His head lowers, his chin draws into his chest, he crouches . . .*
> STANLEY's *body shudders, relaxes, his head drops, he becomes still again, stooped.*

I have not quoted the intervening dialogue, which consists of words imitating the inarticulate sounds Stanley makes and of ironically encouraging questions from Goldberg and McCann.

Clearly, at this juncture, the words are less important than the action, which shows that the central character can no longer use words meaningfully.

The silent killer

Silence has never been a more effective theatrical catalyst than at the end of Eugène Ionesco's *The Killer*, which is like *A Slight Ache* in making a man go on talking into a silence while becoming increasingly unbalanced by his failure to elicit a response from another man, who may exist only inside the imagination.

Like *Macbeth*, *The Killer* illustrates the desolating instability of the relationship between the world inside the mind and the world outside. In both there are powerfully destructive forces, which are seen in the long final soliloquy to be coming together. Ionesco leaves the director free to decide whether the hero, Bérenger, should be talking to himself, alone in the half-light, or whether the Killer should appear. If so, *"he is very small and puny, ill-shaven, with a torn hat on his head and a shabby old gaberdine; he has only one eye, which shines with a steely glitter, and a set expression on his still face; his toes are peeping out of the holes in his old shoes."* He shrugs his shoulders and chuckles softly, but never utters any other sound during Bérenger's speech, which takes up eleven of the script's hundred pages.

Bérenger is walking along a road between the country and the town, where the mysterious Killer has evaded the authorities' halfhearted attempts to hunt him down. The previous action has (intermittently) built up a thrillerlike suspense, which the audience would expect—expectations being based on previous experiences in the theater—to reach its climax in an exciting sequence that will show the Killer being cornered. Perhaps he will be arrested or killed; perhaps he will claim another victim—Bérenger. Ionesco is more concerned to show how the enemy inside joins forces with the enemy outside. Whether the Killer is present or absent, chuckling or silent, Bérenger is talking mainly to the elements in his own disposition that refuse to accept the liberal humanist values that his conscious mind affirms.

The monologue starts confidently. With all the arguments of common sense on his side, Bérenger seems stronger than his adversary in every way. What right does the Killer have to cut off other people's chances of happiness? Does he think happiness is impossible? Is he a pessimist, a nihilist, an anarchist?

Does he hate women? Think the human race is rotten? Or kill out of kindness to spare his victims from the suffering that life has in store for them? Or to cure their fear of death? Or does he hate mankind, believe the existence of the universe to be a mistake?

Getting no reaction, Bérenger threatens that he has law and order on his side. He is beginning to lose his self-control, while his silent adversary seems quite unaffected by his insistence that Christ died on the cross for him, out of love:

> If Christ's not enough for you, I give you my solemn word I'll have an army of saviours climbing new Calvaries just for you, and have them crucified for love of you! . . . They must exist and I'll find them! Will that do?
> (*Chuckle from the* KILLER.)
> Do you want the whole world to destroy itself to give you a moment of happiness, to make you smile just once? That's possible too! I'm ready myself to embrace you, to be one of your comforters; I'll dress your wounds, because you *are* wounded, aren't you? You've suffered, haven't you? You're still suffering? I'll take pity on you, you know that now. Would you like me to wash your feet? Then perhaps you'd like some new shoes? You loathe sloppy sentimentality. Yes, I can see it's no good trying to touch your feelings. You don't want to be trapped by tenderness! You're afraid it'll make a fool of you. You've a temperament that's diametrically opposed to mine. All men are brothers, of course, they're like each other, but they're not always alike. And they've one thing in common. There must be one thing in common, a common language . . . What is it? What is it?

Bérenger has already talked himself into an untenable position. Having baited his hook with the promise that mutual understanding must be possible, he will end by sinking the hook into his own flesh. He concedes that the Killer has the right to deny love and think charity a cheat. But what is the purpose of the killing he does? What use can he make of the fear it wins for him? Bérenger tries to tempt him with offers of money, friendship, introductions to girls. By now he is finding the silence almost intolerable. Like Pinter's characters in *A Slight Ache,* he is helpless to stop it from acting on him like a negative spur, pushing him backward into confession.

Often, I have my doubts about everything too. But don't tell
anyone. I doubt the point of living . . . the meaning of life,
doubt my own values and every kind of rational argument. I
no longer know what to hang on to, perhaps there's no more
truth or charity. But if that's the case, be philosophical; if all
is vanity, if charity is vanity, crime's just vanity too . . . When
you know everything's dust and ashes, you'd be a fool if you
set any store by crime, for that would be setting store by life . . .
That would mean you were taking things seriously . . . and
then you'd be in complete contradiction with yourself.

Can a mouth that says nothing contradict itself? The contradiction is in the words that Bérenger has fed into the silence.
If he goes on talking long enough, he cannot avoid contradict-
ing himself. Not yet realizing that he's trapped himself, he tries
to laugh at the Killer, ridiculing the idealistic belief in crime
that forces him to take all the trouble of killing people without any prospect of deriving benefit from it. The laughter dies
on Bérenger's lips, trumped either by the continuing silence
or the unvarying chuckle. Soon he is kneeling in front of the
Killer, admitting his ignorance.

It's possible that the survival of the human species is of no
importance, so what does it matter if it disappears . . . perhaps the whole universe is no good and you're right to want
to blast it all, or at least nibble at it, creature by creature, piece
by piece . . . or perhaps that's wrong. I don't know anymore,
I just don't know.

Even then, though, while there may be no reason to stop killing, he could still stop without having a reason, and this is what
Bérenger pleads for. Won't he desist just for a month, a week,
forty-eight hours? The Killer's response is to pull out his knife.
Bérenger's immediate reaction is to become extremely aggressive. (If the Killer is invisible, the change is abrupt enough to
show that he has given up all hope of conciliation.) He produces
two pistols from his pocket, aiming at the Killer. But his anger,
fueled only by a chuckle, or by silence, has to run out soon. He
can't shoot. There's nothing he can do, except wait for the end.
    This sequence creates a tremendously powerful theatrical
image, though its only components are an actor (or two) and
an empty stage. The speech is not so much a monologue as a
conversation with the Nothingness, which is given an almost

perceptible existence by the space that surrounds Bérenger. If the actor is (as Hugo von Hofmannsthal once said) "the mask of God, the one who suffers for the others," the Killer is the mask of the void, the one who inflicts the suffering inherent in the human condition. The director's decision about whether he should be physically present or not is only a decision about whether the mask should be visible or invisible.

As with the Ghost in *Hamlet*, Banquo's ghost in *Macbeth*, and the ghosts that appear to Brutus in *Julius Caesar*, the reader's problem is very different from that of the director, who can't have things both ways, as the reader can, letting his imagination shuttle between the alternatives. But, like so many sequences that take full advantage of the medium, Bérenger's speech is far from easy to read. In a generalized way the reader can guess at its theatrical potential as a duet with an unresponsive and possibly nonexistent partner. But it is no easier for him to conjure an impression of an empty space from his visual imagination than an impression of silence from his auditory imagination. Berenger is onstage for a very long time, going through a wide emotional gamut from extreme confidence to extreme desperation, from triumph at cornering the man who killed the girl he loved to suicidal surrender. What would the theatrical effect be like from moment to moment? How much of a mocking echo would the silence give back?

IO

Meaning and experience

*What the writer wrote—What does it mean?—A prenatal
examination—The meaning and the experience—From the root
experience to the collective reaction—The writer's intentions—
What about ideas?—The general and the particular—The
generalized salesman—Waiting for the end—Levels of
communication—Games and gardens*

What the writer wrote

One of the greatest advantages a reader has over audiences is that
he's closer to the writer's original work. Not necessarily closer to
his original conception, which may have been more in the form
of images or emotional tangles than words, but there, printed on
the page, are the words the playwright chose in the order he arranged them. The rhythms that rise up from the page are his
rhythms, unaffected by the director's ideas, the actors' personalities, the designer's way of dividing up the space. If we get the
impression that Hamlet is hesitating, picking his way through a
maze of contrary impulses, this is an illusion thrown up not by an
actor's timing but by Shakespeare's words and rhythms. These can
be squeezed by a bad production into a wrongheaded interpretation; with a new play, unless we can read it for ourselves, we may
find it hard to make up our minds whether production and acting are doing justice to what the writer wrote.

What does it mean?

There is one inescapable difficulty. If we ask ourselves the question "What does it mean?" when we are sitting in an auditorium,
we do not expect the same kind of answer as we do when sitting
in an armchair with a book in our hands, at liberty to stop and
think whenever we like, or to reread a difficult passage. Consider Lucky's speech in Beckett's *Waiting for Godot:*

Given the existence as uttered forth in the public works of
Puncher and Wattmann of a personal God quaquaquaqua
with white beard quaquaquaqua outside time without exten-
sion Who from the heights of divine apathia divine athambia
divine aphasia loves us dearly with some exceptions for reasons unknown but time will tell and suffers like the divine
Miranda with those who for reasons unknown but time will
tell are plunged in torment plunged in fire whose fire and
flames if that continues and who can doubt it will fire the
firmament that is to say blast hell to heaven so blue still and
calm so calm with a calm which even though intermittent is
better than nothing . . .

What this communicates in performance is very different from
what it communicates in print. The audience rapidly abandons
all hope of understanding or even construing what Lucky is trying to say. He has already been onstage for about twenty-five
minutes mutely and slavishly obeying the orders of a bullying
master, who keeps him attached to a rope. After such a protracted
silence, we're taken very much by surprise when he begins to speak.
Nor are we allowed to concentrate on what he is saying. Here are
Beckett's instructions for the behavior of the onstage audience:

(1) VLADIMIR *and* ESTRAGON *all attention,* POZZO *dejected dis-
gusted.* (2) VLADIMIR *and* ESTRAGON *begin to protest,* POZZO'*s suf-
ferings increase.* (3) VLADIMIR *and* ESTRAGON *attentive again.*
POZZO *more and more agitated and groaning.* (4) VLADIMIR *and*
ESTRAGON *protest violently.* POZZO *jumps up, pulls on the rope.
General outcry.* LUCKY *pulls on the rope, staggers, shouts his text.
All throw themselves on* LUCKY *who struggles and shouts his text.*

Lucky would, in any case, probably be speaking too fast for the
audience to form more than a vague idea of what he is saying,
and certainly there is no worry—as there is for the armchair
reader—about where the punctuation would come if there were
any, about who Puncher and Wattmann are, about what *athambia*
means, about whether the Miranda is Miranda in *The Tempest*
(who suffered with those she saw suffer) and about the relative
positions of the fire, the flames, and the firmament. We can tell
ourselves that we aren't meant to be in a position to answer these
questions, but if they intrigue us, why should we stop ourselves
from struggling with them?

Admittedly, they are unusually puzzling, but there are many speeches in the work of playwrights as diverse as Shakespeare, Strindberg, and Stoppard that are not easy to digest immediately, whether we are hearing them or reading them. My point is that in the theater we have no option but to content ourselves with the initial impact. Our intellect is not allowed to work separately from our emotions and our senses. In the quiet of our homes we may have to make a decision about how long we are to spend on solving the mysteries and whether to go out to the nearest reference library for information about Puncher and Wattmann.

A prenatal examination

With a poem or a novel we can argue that it means what it means, irrespective of what its author intended it to mean. We must judge the achievement, which has an objective existence in print. If the work of art is alive, it is alive in its own right.

To read a play is more like conducting a prenatal examination. Every production is a new birth, even if the mother has been dead for centuries. Some mothers are more explicit than others about how they want their children to be staged, but, as Peter Brook has written in his book *The Empty Space,*

> A word does not start as a word—it is an end product which begins as an impulse, stimulated by attitude and behaviour which dictate the need for expression. This process occurs inside the dramatist; it is repeated inside the actor. Both may only be conscious of the words, but both for the author and then for the actor the word is a small visible portion of a gigantic unseen formation. Some writers attempt to nail down their meaning and intentions in stage directions and explanations, yet we cannot help being struck by the fact that the best dramatists explain themselves the least. They recognise that farther indications will most probably be useless. They recognise that the only way to find the true path to the speaking of a word is through a process that parallels the original creative one. This can neither be by-passed nor simplified.

In modern theatrical practice it usually is simplified because the rehearsal period isn't long enough for director and actors to do all the necessary work, even if they are capable of it. Not only are there countless ways of speaking any sentence, there are as many of joining it up with what preceded it: the actor should make his choice after working his way to an understanding of the pressures underneath it. Only then can he judge whether the words are intended to reveal, to edit, to camouflage, or to conceal what is going on inside the character.

But what about the reader? Does he have, ideally, to proceed along a path parallel to the original creative one? If it is true that he cannot properly understand the text without envisaging the impact of a performance, it follows that he needs to know how the words should be spoken. Does that mean he must be able to find his way to the mixture of memories, desires, ideas, beliefs, and intentions that were in the dramatist's mind at the time of writing? Am I saying we should settle down to read Michael Meyer's biography of Ibsen before starting on *Hedda Gabler*? Certainly not. The best evidence of what was in Shakespeare's mind at the time of writing *Hamlet* is the text itself. This is not to say that Shakespeare's opinions about the human condition were identical with his hero's, but that an internal process has surfaced in the words, the silences, the rhythms, and the actions of the play. All we need to know about it can be learned from study of its component parts and the relationships between them.

The meaning and the experience

In "The Dry Salvages" T. S. Eliot wrote:

> We had the experience but missed the meaning,
> And approach to the meaning restores the experience
> In a different form . . .

As we saw when looking at Lucky's speech, the danger for the armchair reader of a play is to have the meaning but miss the experience. Approach to the experience restores the meaning. A play begins in personal experience and its main intention is to convey experience—not necessarily the same, but necessarily not unrelated—to an audience. The reader is like the actor in that he cannot fully enter into what the text is offering unless he can relate it to his own experience. He may be drawing on his previous experience as a reader, on memories of family life and love affairs, and on stories other people have told him about their experience, but the play will make sense to him only if he can take it over from the writer, appropriate it, savor it by empathizing.

Consider the directness of children's participation in the theatrical experience. When they want to scream out to Red Riding

Hood that a wolf is lying in wait for her in her grandmother's bed, it is not because they have ever found a wolf in their own Grannie's bed but because the story links up with other fantasies that have frightened them. At a performance of *Hamlet* there may be no danger of our shouting out a warning that Laertes is fighting with a poisoned rapier, but if we are emotionally involved in the experience, our anxiety is not altogether unlike that of children at a pantomime. Certainly we are feeling something that the armchair reader cannot feel. The ideas of fratricide, incest, and murderously foul play in a duel are not going to work him into a fever of hatred and indignation while he sits quietly looking at superb blank verse in black print on white paper. What he can do and should do is remind himself frequently that Shakespeare was writing for a collective reaction.

From the root experience to the collective reaction

Much of the material a playwright uses derives directly from personal experience, but the private meaning it has for him exists simultaneously in his brain with the public meaning he wants it to acquire in performance. Consider what happens when Hedda Gabler burns Eilert Loevborg's book. Loevborg is a talented, passionate man whom she has rejected, opting to spend her life with the boring Tesman. As a child, Hedda had envied the beautiful hair of another schoolgirl, Thea. Although Thea has since become Loevborg's intimate friend, Hedda, who does not want to become a mother, is less jealous of their physical intimacy than of its productivity. By burning the book she can punish Thea for the part she played in bringing it into existence:

> I'm burning your child, Thea! You with your beautiful, wavy hair! (*She throws a few more pages into the stove.*) The child Eilert Loevborg gave you. (*Throws the rest of the manuscript in.*) I'm burning it! I'm burning your child!

Ibsen's wife, Suzannah, who was fifty-three when he wrote the play, had once been admired for her beautiful hair, and like Hedda, who has decided to reject passion in favor of sedate domesticity, Ibsen had recently decided to stay with his wife instead of traveling around the world with the passionate young girl who was offering herself to him. When he wrote the speech I have just quoted, he was probably thinking simultaneously of the girl, his wife's hair as it used to be and as it was now, of his own decision to stay with her, of his life as it might have been if he had taken the opposite decision, and of the theatrical effect that would be created by the sequence he was writing. He may also have been thinking about why he had only one son. According to one witness, Suzannah had said she would not bear him any more children. So the complex meaning that the text had for him was quite different from the meaning he wanted it to convey in performance.

The writer's intentions

This is one reason for being very careful when we talk about a playwright's intentions. Though the audience would be unable to analyze the ingredients of the book-burning scene Ibsen would probably not have written it as he did if he had not wanted to come to terms with painful private experiences. He may have been feeling guilty about staying unadventurously with his wife, or he may have been partly unconscious of his own reasons for bringing all these themes into his play. Discussions of a playwright's "intentions" usually disregard the fact that the process of writing is largely compulsive.

The involuntary elements in it are not in evidence, so the voluntary ones tend to be exaggerated by biographers, critics, and examination papers. The writer may be more or less in control of the technical and more superficial elements, but he is no more in control of the process by which he creates a play than he is of his personality, or his past life. Heathcote Williams described the experience of writing his play *AC/DC* by saying, "I just happened to be a radio set on a certain circuit." Or, as Pinter put it in a speech at the National Student Drama Festival in 1962, "you arrange *and* you listen, following clues you leave for yourself, through the characters. And sometimes a balance is found, where image can freely engender image and where at the same time you are able to keep your sights on the place where the characters are silent and in hiding. It is in the silence that they are most evident to me."[*]

What about ideas?

In 1895 Bernard Shaw opened his campaign for the "New" Ibsenite theater, "theater as a factory of thought, a prompter of conscience

---

[*]See also page 120 of Ronald Hayman: *Harold Pinter*, Heinemann (UK), 1980 (fourth edition) and Frederick Ungar (US), 1973.

and an elucidator of social conduct." In March 1950 Terence
Rattigan took this statement as his starting point for an attack
on "The Play of Ideas," which he launched in the *New States-
man,* and the controversy lasted till May. James Bridie, Peter
Ustinov, Benn Levy, Sean O'Casey, and finally Shaw himself con-
tributed articles on "The Play of Ideas." Each playwright whipped
up his own mixture of sense and nonsense; Shaw's, of course, was
the most persuasive and the most dangerous. Plays must be all
talk, he said, so how could the talk have no ideas behind it? A fair
debating point, but it does not follow that "The quality of a play
is the quality of its ideas." The ideas in Jean-Paul Sartre's plays
are far superior to the ideas in either Arthur Miller's or Ionesco's,
but their plays are better than his. It isn't the ideas in Shakespeare's
plays that have excited audiences, readers, and scholars all over
the world for nearly four centuries. It is the way they are expressed.

But we should be careful to differentiate between the ideas—
philosophical, political, social, religious—that are tucked explicitly into the dialogue of a play and its overall idea, which may
not be at all explicit. *Idea* is not even the best word; *meaning* is
better but still not ideal. The didactic purpose of a play by Brecht
or Edward Bond is not necessarily identical with what it communicates. Theatrical ideas, images, and rhythms have their own
way of talking to an audience, which does not always accord with
the writer's conscious intention. A condemnation of war and violence may serve partly as a pretext for handling material that is
intrinsically more attractive to the writer than he realizes. His
treatment of it may, despite his intentions, reveal an ambivalence that he cannot control. Here the reader has more freedom
than the director, who may be obliged (if the writer is alive) to
produce a compromise between the play the writer intended to
write and the play he actually wrote. The reader can concentrate entirely on the one he wrote. (If there is a preface, don't
read it until afterward.)

The general and the particular

To interest the public, a play's relevance must extend some distance beyond the private experience of its author, but it is difficult to measure how far *Death of a Salesman* is about selling in
general, or how far *Waiting for Godot* is about the human condition, or how far *The Killer* is about the impotence of liberal
humanism. But these questions must not be ignored.

The generalized salesman

Arthur Miller's play has a lot to say about salesmen in general. Willy's surname is a portmanteau of *low* and *man*, and he is unmistakably a representative of the thousands who earn a living out of sales-talk, without ever quite earning enough to pay off the mortgage on the house they raise their family in. The Willy in the script is sufficiently individualized to make us care about him personally. We can see that he was stupid to commit himself so deeply to the phony values of salesmanship, losing the capacity to discriminate between a line of patter and a serious promise, but we feel sorry for him as we do for a caged leopard. An animal that in different circumstances could be formidable is looking pathetic, and his cubs are growing up in the same imprisoning confusion.

Reading the play we are more aware of the neatly carpentered slots that interrelate so many images of claustrophobia; in performance we are merely exposed to their emotional pressure. The set should make the home look fragile, encircled with solid apartment blocks, dwarfed by angular towers. The play's opening puzzle about Willy's unexpected return is solved when he complains of being incapable of driving beyond Yonkers. He feels boxed in and his mind is playing tricks. He thinks the windows are all shut when they aren't and that he's been driving with the windshield open when it doesn't open on his new car. All these elements in the first act prepare for the knocking sequence, set claustrophobically in a flashback inside a gents' cloakroom, and for Willy's crazy attempt to plant seeds by torchlight in his yard.

Reading the play we are more likely to become aware of the schematic structure by which the brother and the neighbor are set up to incarnate alternative modes of life. In performance they are merely men who seem less likable than Willy, so it is quite understandable when he rejects the opportunities they offer him. Ben, the tough, confident, authoritative brother, who made a fortune in Alaska, has given Willy a chance to escape from the airless city to a pioneering life that could have made him happier and richer. Charley, the kindhearted, law-abiding, wise-cracking neighbor later offers him a job when he is out of work, but he is too proud to accept, though not too proud to go on borrowing money from him. Charley, always skeptical about the popularity that the Loman boys' athletic prowess wins for them, brings his son up very differently. In the flashbacks Bernard is a bookworm; in the present tense he has thrown off this unattractive mask to become a successful lawyer and father, while Biff and Happy are still floundering unhappily in the affairs that follow from impressing girls with a line of talk that is very much like sales-talk. The play's social criticism may be more punchy in performance, but it is clearer in reading. Even the recurrence of the word "dream" in the stage directions works as a reminder that Willy's fantasies are not purely private. The nightmare from which he escapes into suicide is the American Dream.

One advantage of writing social criticism in dialogue form is that you can advance contradictory arguments without needing to make your balance sheet balance. During Miller's restaurant sequence, the waiter comes out with a neat variation on the Marxist point that commerce is a form of theft. A family business is best, he says. "'cause what's the difference? Somebody steals? It's in the family. Know what I mean?" Miller is at an even further remove than his character from explicitly endorsing the Marxist viewpoint, and while a playwright can use this technique defensively to introduce ideas unpalatable to his audience, he can also use it creatively to explore his own ambivalences. The "How do I know what I think till I see what I write?" attitude is still more viable if you are writing dialogue.

Waiting for the end

Waiting for Godot is one of the plays that tend to make people come out of the theater with a strong desire to read the text they have just heard in performance. They have probably felt mystified, intrigued, stimulated by the strange resonance of the stylish dialogue and the curious vagueness of the characters, who are as absentminded about what happened yesterday as they are uncertain about where they are today.

Is it in some sense a religious play? It cannot be accidental that the name Godot is so close to God. Admittedly the play was written in French, and admittedly Godot had already been used as a surname by Balzac; but Beckett, who was brought up in Dublin, would have been unable to write "Godot" without thinking separately of the first syllable. There are also explicit references to the two thieves and the crucifixion, to salvation, to the existence of a personal God with a white beard, to the possibility of comparing oneself with Christ, to the fire and flames of hell, to blessedness, and to Cain and Abel. When the boy says that he thinks Mr. Godot's beard is white, Vladimir's response is "Christ have mercy on us!" After the boy has gone, Estragon asks what would happen if they dropped Godot, and Vladimir answers "He'd punish us." In an interview with Harold Hobson,* Beckett said that he "soon lost faith. I don't think I ever had it after leaving Trinity." But the doctrines and parables that permeated his mind as a child went on to permeate his work. He also told Harold Hobson: "One of Estragon's feet is blessed, and the other is damned. The boot won't go on the foot that is damned; and it will go on the foot that is not. It is like the two thieves on the cross."

Though *Waiting for Godot* is by no means a "play of ideas" in Terence Rattigan's sense, it is constructed around ideas that could be explicated intellectually. In fact they had all been formulated discursively in Beckett's short study of Proust (1931).† That art is the apotheosis of solitude. That there is no communication. That speech is always either falsified by the speaker or distorted by the listener. That our memories of the past are no closer to what actually happened than images produced by our imagination. That neither we nor our ambitions are the same as they were yesterday. That there can be no achievement because the subject can never be identified with the object of his desire. That time doesn't pass but stays around us like a continuum.

The central idea of the play is its ambiguous image of the human condition. The act of waiting is itself a contradictory combination of doing nothing and doing something. We are all trapped between birth and death, condemned to consciousness; Vladimir and Estragon seem to be trapped onstage. Where are they? A country road with a single tree looks more desolate than if there were no trees at all. Is the tree standing in for Nature? Is it the whole earth? There's nothing to force them to stay, but there's nowhere for them to go. The only way out is death, the only relief is night. If they're incapable of suicide or of any other action and if Godot goes on failing to appear, waiting for him is equivalent to waiting for nightfall, for death, or just for the end of the play.

*International Theatre Annual No 1, Calder, (UK), 1956.
†I've analyzed the book's relationship to the play in *Samuel Beckett,* Heinemann (UK), 1980, (third edition) Frederic Ungar (US), 1974.

In *Hamlet,* as in *A Midsummer Night's Dream,* the presence of a play within the play works like a mirror focused in on the theatrical situation. In *Waiting for Godot* the implicit acknowledgement of the audience's presence works in the same way. Are we any less trapped than the actors or the characters? There we are, sitting there, and unless we opt out of it by leaving, we have to wait. Doing nothing or doing something? Waiting for Godot or waiting for the final curtain? This is an aspect that the armchair reader can easily forget. And for the audience in the theater, part of the suspense hinges on the difficulty of guessing how the playwright will manage without the ordinary machinery of suspense. How will he make nothing go on happening for two hours?

Is it a play about nothingness? The single tree and the empty stage play a larger part in the audience's experience than the reader is likely to allow for. The audience will be aware of them all the time; the reader will be reminded of the tree only when Vladimir and Estragon wonder whether they're waiting by the right one, where they arranged to meet Godot; when they try to hang themselves from it; and when they inspect it in Act Two.

Beckett's instincts had been minimalist long before minimalism became fashionable. In *Waiting for Godot* he stripped away most of the ingredients that traditionally constitute drama—suspenseful action, heroic characters, spectacular decor and costumes. He eliminated *coups de théâtre,* and reduced the onstage action to activity that looks almost improvised, though by reading the script you find that the dialogue is constructed with more care, precision, and subtlety than was apparent in the performance.

Levels of communication

Of all Beckett's plays, the most aggressively minimalist—and one of the hardest to understand—is a twelve-minute piece that premiered in 1973. Most of the stage is dark. We see a woman's mouth, brightly lit, higher than we would have expected it to be, and two inches of surrounding flesh. A listening figure is dimly discernible, some way off. Our attention is riveted by movements of tongue, lips, and teeth as semicoherent phrases jab out fragments of information about a female creature expelled prematurely from the womb. She never quite managed to begin living. Her parents had no time for each other or for her. Agitated and breathless, she talks about herself in the third person. Focusing on the mouth and the insistent voice, we learn little about the mind or the body. The play is called *Not I* because she balks at each attempt to talk about herself in the first person. "What? . . . who? . . . no! . . . she!"

The armchair reader of this script might appear to be at an advantage over the theatergoer because the syntax is so dense and ellipitcal that the text would be largely incomprehensible, even if the actress spoke more slowly than Beckett wanted her to. The impact depends less on narrative than on tone, inflection, and audible pain. Through speech—mainly its tone and rhythm—emotional pressure is being exerted on an audience that is intellectually out of its depth.

Should we try to read the script without decoding any more of it than we could in the theater? As with Lucky's speech in *Waiting for Godot,* the armchair reader should penetrate as deeply as he can into the meaning, using dictionaries, reference books, and whatever he needs. But he should never forget that what he's reading is a play. Had Beckett designed *Not I* for radio or television, the reader would need to approach it differently. Since it's written for the theater, he needs to visualize an acting area in which most of the actress and most of the stage are invisible. The stage picture is like a painting in which most of the canvas is black, with one small area of brightness somewhere not in the middle. The apparently wasted space is contributing to the composition. The viewer's reaction would be quite different if the canvas were smaller, or if there were no desert of darkness around the oasis of light. Puzzled and frustrated, the audience is being forced to focus in an unprecedented way on a woman's mouth visible only in long shot. It might have been expected that a close-up view of the mouth would make more impact, but, as we saw when the play was televised, it makes less.

Though the play is reminiscent of minimalist art, Beckett said the only painting directly involved in inspiring it was Caravaggio's *Beheading of St. John the Baptist,* which he saw in Malta about four months before he started writing the play. [James Knowlson, *Damned to Fame: The Life of Samuel Beckett,* London: 1996: 558.]

The isolated mouth may derive from St. John's partially disembodied head, but it also derives from preoccupations that surfaced in Beckett's earlier fiction. In the 1953 novel *The Unnamable,* the narrator talks about a voice

> It issues from me, it fills me, it clamours against my walls, it is not mine, I can't stop it, I can't prevent it. From tearing

me, racking me, assailing me. It is not mine, I have none, I have no voice and must speak, that is all I know.

Using Peter Brook's terms, we could say that in writing *Not I* Beckett was finding a true path to the words that came pouring out of him. This kind of theater is at the opposite extreme from staging a battle or showing the Conquistadores' ascent of the Andes, but the medium can accommodate both kinds of action.

Games and gardens

Game-playing in Stoppard's early plays owes a good deal to Beckett. For the two courtiers in *Rosencrantz and Guildenstern Are Dead*, as for the two tramps in *Waiting for Godot*, enforced idleness becomes a trampoline for conversational bouncing. Rosencrantz and Guildenstern pass time by tossing coins, fabricating arguments, and playing verbal games. They are men who'd have a place only on the edge of heroic drama.

Hamlet is a Copernican play: the throne is as central to the story as the earth was to the universe in the view then prevalent. Stoppard has always been amused by the dizziness that ensues when our map of the cosmos is changed, and it is astonishing to Dottie in his 1976 play *Jumpers* (as it is to Penelope in his 1967 television play *Another Moon Called Earth*) that an astronaut has landed on the moon. "And suddenly everything we live by—our rules—our good, our evil—our ideas of love, duty—all the things we've counted on as being absolute truths—because we filled all existence—they're all suddenly exposed as nothing but local customs—nothing more—because he has seen the edges where we stop."

Stoppard's most fruitful exploration of perspective is in his 1993 play *Arcadia*, which is so ingeniously structured, so richly textured, and so dexterous in manipulating scientific theories that few people—if any—could digest everything in the play without the aid of a script. Probably the best approach to the play is to see a performance, read a script, and then see another performance.

In the same way that a character can be loaded with a dual identity, Stoppard gives the set a double meaning.

The action of the play shuttled back and forth between the early nineteenth century and the present day, always in this same room. Both periods must share the state of the room, without the

additions and subtractions which would normally be expected.
The general appearance of the room should offend neither pe-
riod. In the case of props—books, paper, flowers, etc.,—there is
no absolute need to remove the evidence of one period to make
way for another. However, books, etc., used in both periods should
exist in both old and new versions. The landscape outside, we
are told, has undergone changes. Again, what we see should
neither change nor contradict.

The Derbyshire country house, Sidley Hall, is surrounded by a
large park, and changes in its landscaping reflect changes of style
in the eighteenth and nineteenth centuries. Until about 1740,
the house had a formal Italian garden, but this survived only until
Capability Brown popularized a more "natural" style, sabotag-
ing formality and scattering trees that had been ranked in aven-
ues. The park became "smooth, undulating, serpentine—open
water, clumps of trees, classical boat-house." But, as a well-
informed character points out, "English landscape was invented
by gardeners imitating foreign painters who were evoking classical authors. The whole thing was brought home in the luggage from the grand tour. Here, look—Capability Brown doing
Claude, who was doing Virgil. Arcadia!"

When the play opens in 1809, the park is about to be rede-
signed in the "picturesque" style, which means that Arcadia will
be disrupted into a romantic and artificial chaos—"untamed
nature in the style of Salvator Rosa. It's the Gothic novel expressed in landscape. Everything but vampires." In Jane Austen's
1798 novel *Northanger Abbey*, Catherine Morland, converted by
Mrs. Radcliffe's novels to this form of romanticism, "voluntarily rejected the whole city of Bath as unworthy to make part of
a landscape."

In Stoppard's plot, one of the links between 1809 and 1993 is
a theory evolved by an opportunistic young academic, Bernard
Nightingale, to solve the mystery of Byron's departure from
England shortly after a visit he paid to Sidley Hall. Working
on evidence that isn't conclusive, Bernard argues that he left after
killing a minor poet in a duel. Woven cleverly and funnily between the two periods, the plot gradually reveals what actually
happened in 1809, and how Bernard finds out that his theory
was unrealistically romantic.

For most plays this would be more than enough material,
but Stoppard also incorporates an amusing variation on chaos

theory, introducing a precocious thirteen year old, Thomasina, who grapples, in 1809, with problems that didn't come into focus until the 1970s, when the study of animal populations led to the realization that long-term predictions can't be based on mathematical formulas. She asks her tutor whether God is a Newtonian. "If you could stop every atom in its position and direction, and if your mind could comprehend all the actions thus suspended, and if you were really, *really* good at algebra you could write the formula for all the future."

Nearly two hundred years later, her notes are found by a postgraduate mathematician. What she saw, he says, was that "you can't run the film backwards. Heat was the first thing which didn't work that way. Not like Newton. A film of a pendulum or a ball falling through the air—backwards, it looks the same . . . But with heat, friction, a ball breaking a window . . . You can put back the bits of glass but you can't collect up the heat of the smash. It's gone."

Listening to dialogue like this, many people must have wished they could interrupt the actors. "Excuse me. Would you mind saying that again?" Reading a script, you not only have the advantage of setting your own pace, you also see how much less Stoppard would have achieved by writing essays about landscape gardening, Byron, dueling, and chaos mathematics. *Arcadia* is structured in such a way that each part contributes to the whole. Thomasina's ideas about the possibility of finding a mathematical formula for the future are not irrelevant to Bernard's hypothesis about the past. The tutor who has sex with the nymphomaniac wife of the minor poet is exiled from the house into the purpose-built hermitage that graces the picturesque park. The most sympathetic characters are all unpretentious, like the youngsters and the female journalist. The absurdity of following fashions in landscape design is put into the same perspective as the absurdity of the writer whose anger at being cuckolded is quickly defused by praise for his poetry from his wife's lover.

Stoppard could not have said what he wanted to say without making some of the characters sympathetic and others ridiculous—a point that emerges more clearly from reading the script than from seeing a performance.

II

Photogenic action

Passive acting—Spaces between words—Movies about actors—From place to place—What the camera choses for you—Closing the gap—Swelling veins, big eyes, and small sighs

Reading a screenplay isn't like reading a playscript. In the cinema, words, space, actors, objects, sound, silence, and background are all being manipulated differently by the writer, who may himself be manipulated none too scrupulously by the director. Robert Bolt, who worked with David Lean on *Dr. Zhivago, Lawrence of Arabia,* and *Ryan's Daughter,* found the only way to keep the screenplays intact was to involve Lean in writing them. Some writers have become rich by writing films, but none has become famous, and though well-known playwrights, such as Harold Pinter and Tom Stoppard, have written a lot of screenplays, most filmgoers would be unable to name any of them—or name any other screenwriters. Some of the best films have been made by directors such as Ingmar Bergman, Jean-Luc Godard, and Krysztof Kieslowski, who have written their own scripts.

When you're reading a screenplay, your visual imagination gets more exercise than when you're reading a playscript, since less depends on the words and more on the pictures, most of which you have to supply mentally, even if the book is illustrated with a lot of stills. Nothing can be done about the fact that some people find it easier than others to operate their imagination as if it were a film camera constantly on the move; what's controllable is the amount of effort that goes into visualizing. You can tell yourself when you're zooming into close-up, and you can think about changes of expression, posture, gesture, costume, setting, movement from place to place and from face to face.

The dialogue is no longer the only engine driving the action forward, even when a film is made out of a play such as *Hamlet* or *Who's Afraid of Virginia Woolf?* or *The Night of the Iguana.* The role of the writer skews around—he becomes a purveyor of photogenic action. Shakespeare unwittingly supplied most of the visual ingredients used in the drowning sequence of Olivier's film, and when John Huston was shooting *The Night of the Iguana* from Tennessee Williams's play, he had trouble with a sequence that had been written for the film. The fifteen-year-old Charlotte comes into the bedroom of Shannon, the former priest who's working as a tour guide. Having already had more than enough trouble with girls under the age of consent, he gives reasons for not wanting to make love. Though Huston liked the dialogue, he knew the scene wasn't coming to life, and, asked for advice, Tennessee Williams suggested that the unexpected appearance of the girl should startle Shannon, who's shaving, into knocking over the whisky bottle balanced on the bureau next to the shaving mirror. Insisting that they're not going to make love, he paces about, oblivious of the damage that broken glass is doing to his bare feet. Excited, Charlotte kicks off her shoes and joins him, deliberately walking on shards of broken glass. Action devised by the writer is choreographed by the director, but, as in a ballet, the audience is unaware of any dividing line between devising and choreographing.

Passive acting

In cinema, as in television, the actor is more passive than in the theater. His main function is to be photographed. François Truffaut was only half joking when he defined cinema as the art of photographing beautiful women, and what makes *The Blue Angel* into an unforgettable film is Josef von Sternberg's achievement in editing Marlene Dietrich. He cut out the movements and mannerisms he disliked, cleverly choosing the best bits of footage and pasting them together to produce a series of filmic innuendos depending partly on her legs, partly on her voice, partly on the way he posed her and lit her. The script is not much more than a condensation of Heinrich Mann's novel *Professor Unrat.* (The word "unrat" is roughly equivalent to "shit.")

Even in a masterpiece like Eisenstein's *Ivan the Terrible,* the actors are used like scenery. Most of the effects depend on faces, costumes, beards, makeup, facial expression, grouping, posture, gesture, gesticulation, lighting, and camera angles. Generally, the film gives the impression that the actors didn't move much—it's the camera that always seems to be on the move, and generally, cameras appear to tell the truth because they record actual events, even when the events involve directorial orchestration.

Spaces between words

In the theater it's easy to define the difference between what is performance and what isn't. In cinema, it's not the actors but the director who controls all the spaces between the words. He can lengthen or shorten a pause during the editing, and he can film actors before and after they speak their scripted lines. Jean-Luc Godard's relationship with Anna Karina could be compared to Sternberg's with Dietrich. Both actresses may have recognized the mixture of adoration, frustration, and contempt in the way they were being used, but both submitted. In the 1965 film *Pierrot le Fou*, Jean-Paul Belmondo is never scrutinized by the camera as ruthlessly as Karina. When Ferdinand wants Marianne to say she'll never leave him, she offers casual reassurance, and the camera stays on her. On Marianne or on Karina? She looks down, she looks sideways, she tries looking straight into camera. Her eyes drop.

Godard had been building his films around Karina since 1960. Her native language is Danish, and her French became steadily more fluent, but in 1961, making *Une Femme est une Femme,* he cut all the best takes, saying the worst revealed more of her as a woman. The film includes one in which she corrects herself in midsentence. "Moi, je trouve *con* les femmes modernes qui essaient de limi . . . non, ca va . . . ca va pas? . . . ca va pas?" The good take follows: "Moi, je trouve *con* les femmes modernes qui veulent imiter les hommes." ("I think they're stupid—modern women who act like men.") Karina's insecurity about the line and the language seeps into the aggressiveness of the character, which also derives from insecurity. And Godard enjoyed having her perched precariously between the character and herself.

Should the fluffed line and the actress's questions be printed in the published script? If they find their way into the finished film, are they any less integral to it than dialogue that originates out of improvisation? John Cassavetes, Robert Altman, and Mike Leigh are directors who draw on improvisation, but this doesn't make screenplays of their films less readable than the ones based entirely—or mainly—on script. And what about cuts or additions to the dialogue that was originally scripted? It's commonplace during shooting for cuts to be made, lines altered, and snippets of new material written or improvised. Some published scripts include both sequences that were cut and sequences that were added.

In the theater, even when a play is written for a particular actor or director, the writer's work usually receives more than a single performance. Even plays that have sunk into oblivion had performances that varied slightly from night to night. But unless there is a remake, a screenplay gets only one incarnation, and the published script is like a souvenir. Reading the script of a film you've seen, you find your memory is collaborating with your imagination, and you're making more allowance than you would with a play for the appearance, voice, personality, and style of the actors—especially when they're stars.

Movies about actors

A play is never *about* the leading actor, but the *raison d'être* of a film may center on the star. This could be said of Orson Welles's 1941 film *Citizen Kane*, which was scripted by Herman Mankiewicz. Welles wasn't really entitled to the credit he gave himself as cowriter, but one of the reasons the film is still so powerful is that Mankiewicz, while apparently modeling Kane on the newspaper magnate William Randolph Hearst, was also modeling him on Orson Welles, shrewdly exploiting what they had in common—narcissistic exhibitionism and an unquenchable appetite for popularity. Hearst had panache and theatricality, while Welles, given a sufficiently flamboyant role, played with irresistible relish. As Pauline Kael said, he "makes it possible for us not only to enjoy what he does but to share his enjoyment in doing it. . . . Without Orson Welles's physical presence—the pudgy, big prodigy who incarnates egotism—*Citizen Kane* might . . . have disintegrated into vignettes. We feel that he's making it all happen. Like the actor-managers of the old theater, he's the man onstage running the show, pulling it all together." [*The Citizen Kane Book,* London: Secker and Warburg 1971.]

Those who read the script without having seen the film will recognize that it's exceptionally well written—soundly constructed, with a lot of powerful climaxes and amusing lines, some of them derived from true stories that were circulating about Hearst. But it would be as hard to assess the power of Welles's

performance from a mere reading of the script as to picture
Henry Irving in action from reading *The Bells*.

Readers of a screenplay must be divided into two kinds—
those who've seen the film and those who haven't. If you haven't,
you activate your imagination almost as if it were a camera that
has to construct the pictures it shoots, and instead of following
the action through the words, you let the script form a series of
pictures and sounds in your mind.

From place to place

Your powers of visualization are being challenged more keenly
when reading a screenplay than they would be by a playscript or
a novel. Drama has moved a long way since classicism imposed
unity of time, place, and action, but playwrights usually ration
themselves to a minimum of scene changes. Once you've formed
an impression of the Prozorovs' drawing room in *Three Sisters*,
you may have to remind yourself not to let the mental picture
fade, but you can go on using it till the end of the first act.

Novelists and filmmakers can both move effortlessly from one
locale to another, but, communicating directly with readers, the
novelist can guide their attention to the right detail at the right
moment, introducing unobtrusive visual stimuli whenever they
seem necessary. But a reader of screenplays may have to cope
with a passage like:

> *Country road.* GELSOMINA *following three musicians, in step with
> the music. Dissolve.*
>
> *Scene in a small town. A procession is passing. Dusk. Voices sing-
> ing liturgical music.*
>
> L. S. [long shot] *Details of the procession: crucifix, holy images,
> saints, a priest blessing the crowd.*
>
> M. S. [medium shot] GELSOMINA *in the crowd, her eyes wide open
> in beatific admiration of the religious insignia.*
>
> L. S. *entire piazza.*
>
> L. S. *interior of church. Church bells. Dissolve.*
>
> *Exterior. Night. Man on rope. Piazza in town at night.*
>
> *Rain of applause.*

C. U. [close-up] ANNOUNCER (*through loudspeaker*): In a moment Matto will perform the most dangerous of his stunts.
Walking forty meters above the ground, he will eat a dish of
spaghetti.

In this sequence from Federico Fellini's 1954 film *La Strada*, the
simple-minded Gelsomina, whose mother has sold her for ten
thousand lire to a brutish street-performer, is about to meet the
one man who's kind to her, Matto, an acrobat. Readers have to
work quite hard if they are going to form adequate impressions
of the country road, the procession, the piazza, and the church,
while thinking about the sound track, which moves from the
street musicians to the procession before the silence inside the
church is broken by the noise of bells. Even when you've tried
to construct or reconstruct the experience of seeing this bit of
the film, you still have to work out why Fellini introduces a religious perspective before the acrobat makes his first appearance,
eating spaghetti on the high wire against a background of artificial stars. To Gelsomina as she stares admiringly upward, he'll
look like an angel.

What the camera chooses for you

If you're used to playscripts, the main adjustment you have to
make for screenplays is to the different use of space. Unlike the
acting area in a theater, the screen is two-dimensional, and the
audience has less choice in the cinema than in the theater about
where to look. Instead of being free to let your eye wander from
actor to actor and from foreground to background, you see the
end-product of an elaborate process that started on location or
in a studio and ended in a cutting room. The cameras have
moved, sometimes tracking, sometimes dollying. The focus has
varied—close-up, long shot, medium shot—and what the characters seem to be looking at will not always be what the actors
were looking at when the sequence was shot. In the cinema,
following the story and watching a seamless succession of images, you wouldn't have time to work out how these results were
achieved, even if you wanted to.

While film directors can make us look at whatever they want
us to see, directors in the theater have to focus our attention at
different moments on different areas of the relatively large space
that's occupied by the set. An actor can move upstage, a clock

can start chiming, the lighting can change, characters can look upward or upstage or wherever the director wants the audience to look.

On the two-dimensional screen, as in a painting or a photograph, three dimensions are represented, but so is a great deal of movement. Since the camera can go anywhere, the screen-writer is never restricted in the way Ibsen was in *Rosmersholm* when he had to let Mrs. Helseth look through a window to tell the audience that John Rosmer and Rebecca West were drowning themselves in the mill-race.

Film can offer incessant movement not only from one place to another but from one viewpoint to another. In the theater your empathy with the characters does not depend on sharing their viewpoint, but during a love scene in a film, cutting from close-up to close-up, the camera can trick you into sharing the man's view of the woman and hers of him. We may not feel what they feel or think what they think, but we don't just hear what they say—we see what they see.

Closing the gap

We can also be given a privileged view of both lovers at moments when neither can see the other.

> JULIE *reaches for the telephone and this time punches out the number from memory, automatically. We hear* OLIVIER'*s voice.*
>
> JULIE: It's me. I've finished. You can pick it up tomorrow morning. Or today, if you're not too tired.
>
> *Intercut with* OLIVIER'*s flat. Night.*
>
> OLIVIER: I'm not tired. But I won't pick the score up.
> JULIE: (*off*) What?
> OLIVIER: I won't pick it up. I've been thinking about it all week. This music can be mine. A bit too heavy and awkward perhaps, but mine. Or yours, but we've got to make it clear.
>
> JULIE *remains silent, stunned by this piece of news.*
>
> OLIVIER: Are you there?
>
> *Int* JULIE'*s flat. Night.*
>
> JULIE: Yes, you're right.

JULIE *puts the phone down without saying goodbye. She gets up from the table quite abruptly and moves across the room. She goes back, takes a packet of Marlboro from her bag, lights a cigarette, and immediately, barely having lit it, stubs it out in the ashtray. She goes to the kitchen, searches for something on the shelf and finds a flower vase. She fills it with water and stands it on the table. Some blue flowers, still wrapped in cellophane, lie in the hall.* JULIE *unwraps the cellophane and puts the flowers in the water. She smiles faintly at what she has just done, and reaches for the phone again. She redials the number she had punched out a moment ago.* OLIVIER *answers.* JULIE *speaks without preliminaries, but also without the previous sternness or hardness.*

JULIE: Olivier, it's me again. I wanted to ask you . . . Is it true
    that you're sleeping on the mattress . . . ?
OLIVIER: (*off*) Yes.
JULIE: You never told me.
OLIVIER: (*off*) No.
JULIE: Do you still love me?
OLIVIER: (*off*) I do.
JULIE: Are you alone?
OLIVIER (*off*) Of course I'm alone.
JULIE: I'm coming over.

She replaces the receiver. She puts on her coat and scarf.

This is the emotional turning point in Kieslowski's *Blue*. After losing her composer husband and her child in a car crash, Julie has collaborated with Olivier on completing an unfinished score, but has kept him at a distance until his integrity finally softens her resistance. In the theater, a sequence like this could be staged only awkwardly, using different parts of the stage to represent different locales.

Films have often shown both sides of a telephone conversation, but until car telephones and cell phones were invented, it was impossible to film a conversation that started with two people in different places and ended with them together. This is what happens in Quentin Tarantino's 1994 film *Pulp Fiction* in a late-night sequence after Mia, wife of the gang boss Marsellus Wallace, gives herself an overdose of cocaine. With her comatose body in his car, the hit man Vincent, who was taking her out for the evening on his boss's orders, telephones the drug dealer, Lance, who sold him the cocaine. What she needs is a shot of adrenaline, and though Lance has some, he does all he can over the telephone to stop Vincent from coming to the house. Knowing he'll be killed if Mia dies, Vincent refuses to be put off, and just as Lance rings off, Vincent drives onto his lawn and crashes into his house. He's looking out of a window that shatters from the impact.

Like the novel, but unlike the play, film can combine movement in space with movement in time, as it does in *Jules and Jim*.

> *Close-up of* CATHERINE *sitting against the tree, then a long shot of the two men standing over her.*
>
> JIM: We must move on.
> CATHERINE: No, this time I won't move. I give up.
> JULES and JIM: Come on . . . Come on.
>
> *They pick her up, and, linking hands to form a chair, carry her off towards the house. Slow dissolve to a shot of* CATHERINE *on another day, running towards the clothes-line in the garden of the house, on which three swimming costumes are drying. She takes them down.*
>
> CATHERINE: Hey, boys . . . Come and help.
>
> JULES *and* JIM *appear; she presents them with their costumes and they each take a bicycle and ride off. Group shot of the three of them riding along a road.* JIM *is in front, but* CATHERINE *soon catches him up.* JULES *pedals more slowly behind them. Series of different shots as they ride together to the beach: sometimes they are far apart, at other times they ride unhurriedly side by side; most often* CATHERINE *races ahead while* JULES *and* JIM *pedal together. Dissolve to the beach. The two men emerge from the sea in swimming costumes and run laughing towards* CATHERINE, *who is lying on the sand under a sunshade.*

Incidental music is rarely mentioned in scripts, but Georges Delerue's theme tune, which seemed to mingle with the sunlight and the charming insouciance of Jeanne Moreau, Oscar Werner, and Henri Serre, will seep back into the memory of anyone who has seen the film. Those who read *Jules and Jim* without having seen it may find themselves drawing on memories of their own seaside holidays.

Swelling veins, big eyes, and small sighs

Easily accommodating big movements in space and time, cinema can also focus on small details. The screenplay for Ingmar
Bergman's 1955 film *Smiles of a Summer Night* tells us at one
point that a vein swells on the temple of the aggressive Count
Malcolm, who has just arrived in the bedroom of his mistress
to find that his dressing gown and his nightcap are being worn
by another man—the lawyer Fredrik Egerman. There's nothing to stop readers from moving their imagination closer to
an actor's face than it would ever need to go when they're reading a playscript.

   The next day, the Count calls on his wife, Charlotte, who
knows about his infidelity. She does not complain, but expresses
her feelings by playing with his pistols, which are loaded, and
shooting at targets we cannot see. When she asks whether he's
jealous of Egerman's young wife, Anne, who probably knows
nothing about her husband's escapades, Malcolm

   is suddenly furious, but his large eyes are calm.

   MALCOLM: I can tolerate my wife's infidelity, but when
      anyone touches my mistress, I become a tiger. Good
      morning!

   He kisses her fingers and closes the door behind him. CHARLOTTE
   *raises the pistol and fires at the mirror on the door, splintering it
   into a thousand pieces.*

The reader knows that the large eyes of the angry man and the
splinters of glass are in much clearer focus on the screen than
they could be on the stage.

   The possibility of close-up allows silence to be used on-screen
differently from the way it's used in the theater. When Anne
goes into her husband's room, they having nothing to say to each
other.

   *In the big dark room—the shades are drawn—diligence and cigar
   smoke prevail.* FREDRIK *sits in a high-backed chair at a large table
   cluttered with books and papers. He puffs on a fat cigar and wears
   a pince-nez, which makes his face somewhat unfamiliar.* ANNE
   *walks quietly up to her husband, takes the cigar out of his mouth
   and creeps into his lap. She puts her arms round his neck and presses
   her cheek against his chin.*

FREDRIK *patiently allows himself to be fondled and caresses the girl on her back and shoulders. Carefully he gropes for his cigar and takes a puff so that it won't go out.* ANNE *looks at him, smiles sadly, struggles to her feet and starts towards the door with a bowed head.*

FREDRIK: Did my little girl want anything in particular?
ANNE: No, nothing. Forgive me if I disturbed you.

The only thing she can see is the back of a large chair and a cloud of smoke. She closes the door silently, and for the third time finds herself alone in the drawing room.

With a small sigh of sadness and desertion she walks up to the canary cage and stands for some moments looking at the birds hopping from perch to perch.

Then she sits down at her small sewing table and reaches for the embroidery frame.

The silence around her is complete.

The clock on the rococo bureau strikes ten.

The sequence establishes more about the isolation of both husband and wife than it could if they talked to each other. The point is that they can't talk, and the chiming of the clock works like punctuation on the silence, ending it. But this sequence would work no better in the theater than it would in the film if Bergman had made the mistake of shooting the whole of it in a long shot.

Play-reading as a pleasure

Hazel-colored hair—To sum up

Hazel-colored hair

The interest of the public in reading scripts is a relatively new phenomenon. Bernard Shaw had been writing plays for eighteen years before he found a publisher for them. "The English people had for a whole century absolutely refused to read plays," he wrote in a letter to his German translator, Siegfried Trebitsch, in 1903. "I then set to work to make plays readable." Instead of listing the characters at the beginning of the published script, he introduced each one on his first entrance with a description "as elaborate . . . as those of Tolstoy and Turgenev." He boycotted all the technical terms of the theater, not even allowing himself an "Enter" or an "Exit," and he provided lengthy, leisurely stage directions containing the most detailed specifications. Describing John Tanner in *Man and Superman*, he wrote:

> a certain high chested carriage of the shoulders, a lofty pose of the head, and the Olympian majesty with which a mane, or rather a huge wisp, of hazel-colored hair is thrown back from an imposing brow, suggest Jupiter rather than Apollo. He is prodigiously fluent of speech, restless, excitable (mark the snorting nostril and the restless blue eyes, just the thirty-secondth of an inch too wide open), possibly a little mad.

This is not written for the director, who is not going to worry about Greek gods or hazel-colored hair when he casts the part, or for the actor, who is not going to calculate how wide his eyes are open when he plays it, but for the reader, who needs both to be entertained and to be encouraged to visualize with a maximum of precision.

In the letter to Trebitsch, Shaw claimed that "one of the most important things I have done in England is to effect a reform in the printing of plays." He certainly did more than any other playwright toward reinstating the drama with the reading public, and the habit of play-reading has since become even more widespread than it was when he died in 1950. Successful playwrights today can easily find a publisher, and the most successful plays may go on selling at the rate of fifteen thousand to twenty-five thousand copies a year.

When John Arden's play *Serjeant Musgrave's Dance* was produced at the Royal Court in 1959, it played to almost empty houses. Though it has since been staged by Peter Brook in Paris, revived at the Royal Court and by repertory companies, it cannot have been seen in performance by more than a few thousand people, while perhaps a hundred thousand copies of the printed edition have been sold, many to libraries, which probably means that the play has been read by at least a hundred times as many people as have seen it on the stage.

But the contemporary playwright has not copied Shaw's practice of attempting to communicate directly with his readers. Stage directions are still printed with almost telegraphic economy, and the fact that readers are not deterred proves that they are quite willing to use their imagination.

To sum up

Everything I have said in this book could be summed up in the sentence "Imagine a performance as vividly as you can." In the cultural situation we are now in, television is one of many pressures that tend to make us use our imagination less. It is easier to tune in to a serial than to read a play. But when we do—as when we listen to a play on the radio—we find that there is great pleasure to be derived from allowing our imagination to do the work of contributing all the visual elements.

Please skip the remainder of this chapter if you don't like repetition. Nor do I want my résumé of such practical advice as there is in the eleven previous chapters to sound like commandments. But for those who would like to have a summary of it, here it is:

1. Try to remind yourself of what the set might look like, what sort of atmosphere it would evoke, how the action

would fill the space, how the impacts—separately or simultaneously—would affect the audience. Read all stage directions especially carefully.

2. With sound effects, try to imagine the quality of the sound and the way it might help the development toward a climax.

3. Try to make your mind as receptive as possible to the growth of the play's rhythms and the relationships between them.

4. Don't take the words at their face value. Their main function may be to make it possible to reach through them to what lies underneath.

5. Try to think less in terms of character than of identity and of the way it is presented physically.

6. Never psychoanalyze the motivations of the characters as if they were real people.

7. Take time to explore the ambiguities of a script and don't try to close questions the playwright wants to remain open. You *can* have it both ways.

8. Explore and exploit all the opportunities of mental theater. The best actors and the best-equipped theaters in the world all have their limitations. Your imagination can do everything you allow it to. Be generous with it.

9. Look out for the silences, whether they're signposted by stage directions or not. Unanswered questions, ignored requests, broken blank-verse lines, and changes of tone are no less significant than *"Pause"* or *"Silence."*

10. A play does not always mean what the writer means it to mean. The meaning is the resultant force that emerges from the words, the silences, and all the other elements, and from all the relationships that develop between them.

Key to extracts

For the plays, the date in brackets is that of the original performance. The other date is that of the publication.

Page

12   From William Carlos Williams, *Paterson Books 1–5*, MacGibbon and Kee, 1964, p. 165.

14   Anton Chekhov, *Three Sisters* (1901), tr. Ronald Hingley, *The Oxford Chekhov, Vol. 3*, and Oxford Paperbacks *Ivanov, The Seagull, There Sisters*.

17   William Shakespeare, *Hamlet* (*c.* 1601), V, ii. Stage directions between lines 279 and 356.

20   William Shakespeare, *Macbeth* (*c.* 1606), II, i.

20   ibid., II, i, 62–4.

21   ibid., II, ii, 58–63 and 74.

22   ibid., II, iii, 1–4.

23   Arthur Miller, *Death of a Salesman* (1949), *Collected Plays*, Cresset Press, 1958, pp. 205–6.

26   Alfred Lord Tennyson, "The Lady of Shalott."

26   Robert Browning, "The Last Ride Together."

27   Shakespeare, *As You Like It* (*c.* 1600), V, ii, 76–81.

28   Chekhov, *The Cherry Orchard* (1904), tr. Ronald Hingley, *The Oxford Chekhov, Vol. 3*, and Oxford Paperbacks *Uncle Vanya, The Cherry Orchard, The Wood Demon*, p. 112.

28   Edward Albee, *The Zoo Story* (1960), Dramatists Play Service Inc., pp. 22–3.

31   Harold Pinter, *Plays: One*, Methuen Paperbacks, 1976, p. 14.

31   Chekhov, *The Cherry Orchard*, pp. 108–10.

33   August Strindberg, *The Father* (1887), tr. Michael Meyer, Methuen Paperbacks, 1976, pp. 71–2.

36   Bertolt Brecht, *The Life of Galileo* (1943), tr. Desmond I. Vesey, Eyre Methuen, 1963, pp. 71–2.

40   Shakespeare, *Measure for Measure* (*c.* 1604), V, i, 321–31 and 347–51.
42   Nikolai Gogol, *The Government Inspector* (1836), tr. Edward O. Marsh and Jeremy Brooks, Methuen, 1968, pp. 43–4.
45   Oliver Goldsmith, *She Stoops to Conquer* (1773), in *Four English Comedies*, Penguin, 1950, pp. 256–7.
47   Brecht, *The Good Person of Szechwan* (1943), tr. John Willett, Eyre Methuen, 1965, pp. 52–4.
50   Shakespeare, *Macbeth*, I, vii, 55–9.
52   Shakespeare, *King Henry IV Part 1* (*c.* 1598), III, iii, 29–35.
52   ibid., II, iv, 264–70.
53   Shakespeare, *King Henry IV Part 2*, V, v, 48–64.
54   ibid., 89–91.
57   Shakespeare, *Julius Caesar* (c. 1600), III, ii, 13–16 and 83–4.
58   Henrik Ibsen, *Hedda Gabler* (1891), tr. Michael Meyer, Eyre Methuen, 1974, pp. 58–60.
60   ibid., p. 49.
63   Ibsen, *Rosmersholm* (1887), tr. R. Farquharson Sharp, *The Pretenders, Pillars of Society* and *Rosmersholm*, Everyman, 1913, pp. 315–16.
64   Shakespeare, *Hamlet*, IV, vii, 165–182.
67   Pinter, *The Caretaker* (1960), Methuen, 1960, pp. 11–12.
69   Shakespeare, *Hamlet*, I, ii, 115–21.
70   Shakespeare, *Measure for Measure*, V, i, 437–41.
70   ibid., III, i, 106–110.
72   Chekhov, *The Cherry Orchard*, p. 99.
73   Ibsen, *Hedda Gabler*, pp. 108–9.
76   Pinter, *The Birthday Party* (1958), *The Birthday Party and Other Plays*, Methuen, 1960, pp. 85–6 and 87.
79   Eugène Ionesco, *The Killer* (1959), *Plays, Vol. III*, John Calder, 1960, p. 104.
83   Samuel Beckett, *Waiting for Godot* (1953), Faber, 1956, p. 42.
84   Peter Brook, *The Empty Space*, MacGibbon and Kee, 1968, pp. 12–13.
85   T. S. Eliot, *Four Quartets*, Faber.
86   Ibsen, *Hedda Gabler*, p. 99.
87   Pinter, *Plays: One*, p. 14.
91   Beckett, *International Theatre Annual No. 1*, Calder.
93   Samuel Beckett, *The Unnamable*.
94   Tom Stoppard, *Arcadia*.

101 Federico Fellini, *La Strada.*
103 Krystof Kieslowski, *Blue.*
104 Quentin Tarantino, *Pulp Fiction.*
106 Ingmar Bergman, *Smiles of a Summer Night.*
106 Ibid.
108 Bernard Shaw, *Man and Superman* (1905), Penguin, 1946,
     p. 47.